LIVING THROUGH

THE CIVIL WAR

Bob Rees

Chicago, Illinois

www.capstonepub.com
Visit our website to find out more information about Heinemann-Raintree books.

To order:
☎ Phone 888-454-2279
Visit www.capstonepub.com to browse our catalog and order online.

Edited by Andrew Farrow and Megan Cotugno
Designed by Steve Mead
Original illustrations © Capstone Global Library Ltd
Picture research by Ruth Blair
Production by Eirian Griffiths
Originated by Capstone Global Library Ltd
Printed and bound in the USA

15 14 13 12 11
10 9 8 7 6 5 4 3 2 1

Library of Congress Cataloging-in-Publication Data
Rees, Bob.
The Civil War / Bob Rees.
p. cm.—(Living through. . .)
Includes bibliographical references and index.
ISBN 978-1-4329-5996-8 (hb)—ISBN 978-1-4329-6005-6 (pb) 1. United States—History—Civil War, 1861-1865—Juvenile literature. I. Title.
E468.R425 2012
973.7—dc22 2011018258

Acknowledgments
The author and publishers are grateful to the following for permission to reproduce copyright material:
Akg-images pp. 33, 53, 61 (North Wind Picture Archives), 15, 19, 41, 51, 53; Corbis pp. 30, 34, 49 (© Bettmann), 45 (© Medford Historical Society Collection), 25, 29, 47, 54; Getty Images pp. 59 (Alexander Gardner/ George Eastman House), 8 (Fotosearch), 17 (Mathew B. Brady/Library Of Congress/ Time Life Pictures), 26, 64 (MPI); Library of Congress pp. 38 (Kurz & Allison), 13 (Whitechurch, Robert, 1814-ca. 1880, engraver), 20, 55; Mary Evans pp. 27, 43; The Art Archive p. 9 (Culver Pictures); The Johnson Collection/ William Dickinson Washington (1833-1870) The Burial of Latane, 1864 p. 57

Cover photograph reproduced with permission of akg-images.

We would like to thank Jay Williams for his invaluable help in the preparation of this book.

CONTENTS

Some words are printed in bold, **like this**. You can find out what they mean by looking in the glossary.

Some of the first-hand accounts in this book have been edited to make them more understandable.

A WAR OF BROTHER AGAINST BROTHER

In 1860 the United States was a bitterly divided nation. There were strong divisions between the northern and southern halves of the country, both of which had different economies and traditions. Two main political parties dominated politics in the United States at the time. The Republicans largely supported northern interests, while the Democrats largely supported southern interests. Relations between the two parties were getting increasingly bitter by 1860, especially over the issues of slavery and states' rights.

A story of two brothers

In 1862 two brothers fought on opposite sides during the same Civil War battle, without knowing that they were within a few feet of each other. James and Alexander Campbell were from a Scottish family. Alexander lived in New York City, but his brother James had settled in Charleston, South Carolina. Each supported the state where he lived, and so they fought on opposite sides in the Battle of Secessionville, in June 1862. They wrote to each other after the battle.[1]

As tensions reached a boiling point in 1860 and early 1861, 11 southern states **seceded**, or broke away, from the rest of the United States. The Civil War then broke out, lasting from 1861 until 1865. The war was fought between the North, commonly called the **Union**, and the South, commonly called the **Confederacy**. The war's results and consequences have affected people in the United States ever since.

THE HUMAN TOLL

The Civil War is sometimes called "A War of Brother Against Brother," because members of many families fought on opposite sides. The war involved 3.25 million soldiers and sailors. Huge numbers of **civilians** were also caught up in the war. In total over 600,000 people died from both sides, and more than 400,000 were wounded. There have never been greater losses in any war in U.S. history.[2]

The Union flag was made up of 13 stripes, representing the original **colonies**, and 35 stars, representing the 35 states that were part of the United States at the time—including those that had seceded.

The Confederacy changed its flag several times. The original "Stars and Bars" flag (left) caused confusion in battles, since it looked too much like the Union flag. It was replaced by the "Stainless" flag (bottom), but its white background looked too much like a flag of surrender. A red vertical stripe was added to the "Stainless" flag in 1865. Many people believe that the red flag with a blue diagonal cross and white stars was the Confederate flag, but it never was. Rather, it was simply a flag used during army battles.[3]

Did you know?

It is a fascinating fact that, even though the Civil War was fought between 1861 and 1865, there were some survivors who lived on into the second half of the 20th century. The last known Union veteran, Albert Woolson, died in 1956, at the age of 109. The last known **Confederate** veteran, Pleasant Crump, died in 1951, at the age of 104. Some people have claimed that other survivors have lived longer, but their stories are doubted.[4]

BUILDUP TO WAR

By the mid-19th century, the United States stretched from the Atlantic Ocean in the East to the Pacific Ocean in the West. In 1803, as part of an exchange known as the Louisiana Purchase, the United States had bought a huge area of land in the center and southern parts of the country from France. It had won land in the West from Mexico as a result of the Mexican-American War (1846–48).[1]

Over the course of the 1800s, settlers from the original 13 colonies had spread westward in search of land and a new way of life. They had crossed the natural barriers of the Appalachian Mountains in the East and the Rocky Mountains in the West. The Great Plains, in the center, had been called the Great American Desert, because people believed that nobody could live there. But when farmers learned to cultivate the land there, the Plains became the hugely rich agricultural heart of the nation. The American people believed that the occupation of all the land from the East to the West was the nation's "Manifest Destiny," or predetermined right.[2]

By the mid-19th century, large cities had grown up in some places, especially northeastern states, where **industry** was developing. The population was growing quickly, aided by large numbers of immigrants, mostly from Europe.

The impact of geography

Since the country was so large by the mid-19th century, this meant that the war would be fought in very different landscapes. Sometimes large distances were involved. Because the North had a well-developed railroad system and fleets of riverboats, it would have a much easier time moving its troops and supplies.

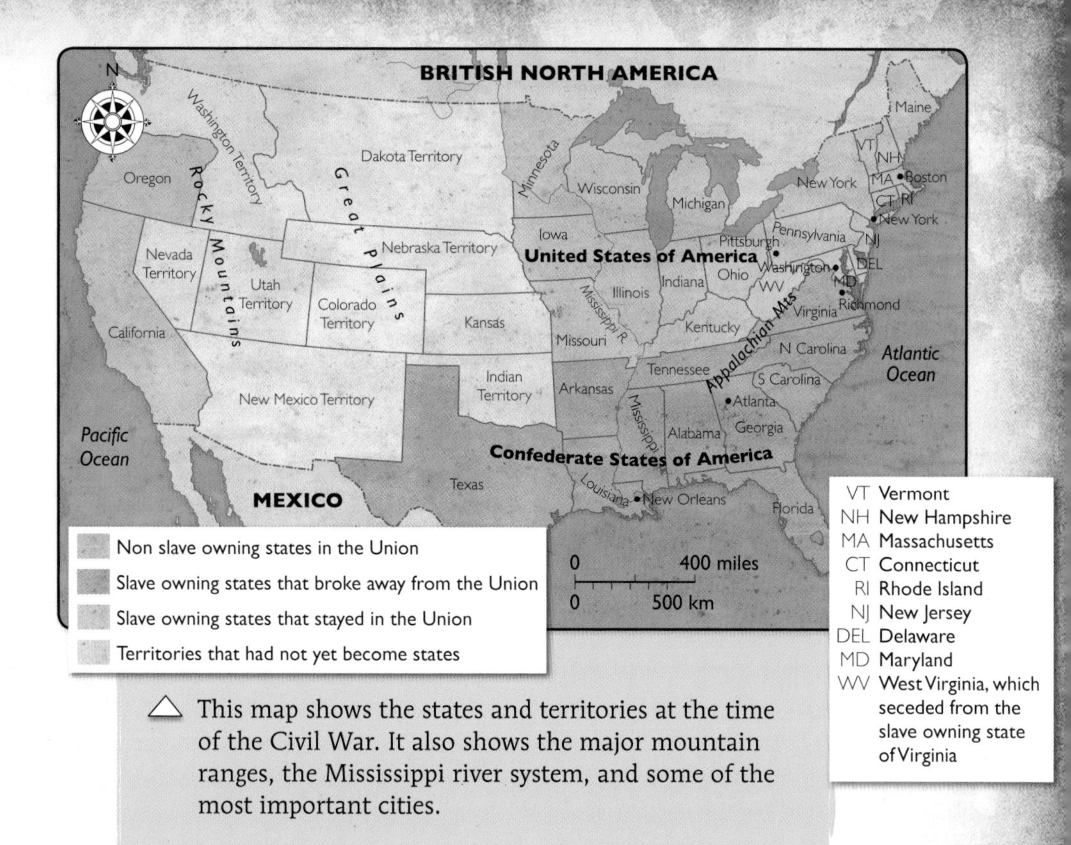

△ This map shows the states and territories at the time of the Civil War. It also shows the major mountain ranges, the Mississippi river system, and some of the most important cities.

THE ECONOMY IN THE MID-19TH CENTURY

The North and South had very different economies by the mid-19th century. In the North, industry developed alongside agriculture, and goods were manufactured for sale. West of the Appalachian Mountains there was agriculture, with **surpluses** being sold to other parts of the United States and to Europe. In the South, people grew food for their own consumption, mostly on small farms. But the economy really depended on the large-scale production of **plantation** crops like cotton and tobacco. Slaves worked on these plantations. These crops were **exported**, mainly to Great Britain, which was growing richer from its cloth factories.

In reality these two systems were different, but they each depended on the other for prosperity. The economy became part of political arguments between the North and South. Northern politicians wanted taxes on **imported** goods. This would benefit the North's iron industry, making its goods the cheapest and thus the most in demand. Southern politicians wanted free trade. This would allow them to export their cotton more easily and make more money.

SLAVES

Since the 16th century, slaves had been forcibly taken from Africa to go to the Americas. They were shipped across the Atlantic in horrifying conditions and then sold. They spent the rest of their lives working. By 1860 there were about four million slaves in the South, and they were very valuable property. However, slavery was not allowed in most northern states.

Slaves had no rights. They were not allowed to marry—although many were used as "breeders" to produce children, who provided more cheap labor. Slaves could not prevent their children from being sold to other slave owners. Slaves received food and shelter but no money for their work. They could not own property. They also could not protect themselves against a slave owner's brutality. Beatings, rape, burning, and exposure were all used against slaves if they displeased their owners.

While most slaves worked in the fields, some worked as "house" slaves. They carried out tasks like cooking, cleaning, and carriage driving. Others worked as craftspeople, such as carpenters, blacksmiths, and fishermen.

△ These slaves were working on a cotton plantation in the 1860s.

FREE BLACKS

Some slaves were freed after fighting for the American colonies during the Revolutionary War (1775–83), and some were able to buy their freedom with money they earned by selling items they created.

Others fled from the South to the North. In the first 60 years of the 19th century, up to 100,000 slaves escaped. Some were helped by people who ran the "Underground Railroad," a network of secret routes and safe places to stay while slaves traveled to the free states in the North or to Canada. These "conductors" included **abolitionists** and other escaped slaves.

Even in the free states, however, there was **segregation**. This meant that black and white people lived separately and black people were **discriminated** against.

THE ABOLITION MOVEMENT

By the mid-19th century, an increasing number of people believed that slavery was **immoral**. Abolitionist groups like the American Anti-Slavery Society, led by William Lloyd Garrison, called for the **abolition** of slavery. Some people, including Garrison, the freed slave Frederick Douglass (see pages 10-11), and Harriet Tubman (see box) demanded instant abolition. Others wanted the gradual end of slavery.

The abolition movement was based largely in the North. This was a big issue that was increasingly dividing the North and South in the prewar period. Over time, southern politicians came to identify northern politics with the abolition movement.[3]

BIOGRAPHY

Harriet Tubman

c. 1820–1913

BORN: Dorchester County, Maryland

ROLE: Abolitionist

Harriet Tubman's parents were slaves, so she was born a slave. In 1849 she ran away and became a **fugitive** slave. She joined the Underground Railroad as a "conductor," helping over 300 people to escape to the North. She was a passionate abolitionist who knew many prominent people. During the Civil War, she was a nurse, a spy, and an army guide. After the war she fought for women's rights and women's right to vote.[4]

SLAVE MEMOIRS

We know a lot about slaves' lives because some slaves wrote about their memories and their experiences. The following are extracts from some famous **memoirs**.

HARRIET JACOBS

Born a slave, Harriet Jacobs escaped and became a supporter of the abolition movement. This is a passage from Jacobs's autobiography, *Incidents in the Life of a Slave Girl* (1861). Here, Jacobs describes the cruelties of a slave owner:

There was a planter who was an ill-bred, uneducated man, but very wealthy. He had six hundred slaves, many of whom he did not know by sight. His extensive plantation was managed by well-paid ***overseers****. There was a jail and a whipping post on his grounds; and whatever cruelties were perpetrated there, they passed without comment. He was so effectually screened by his great wealth that he was called to no account for his crimes, not even for murder.*

Various were the punishments resorted to. A favorite one was to tie a rope round a man's body, and suspend him from the ground. A fire was kindled over him, from which was suspended a piece of fat pork. As this cooked, the scalding drops of fat continually fell on the bare flesh.[5]

FREDERICK DOUGLASS

In his autobiography, *The Life and Times of Frederick Douglass* (1882), Frederick Douglass describes the experience of freedom in the North:

I have often been asked, how I felt when first I found myself on free soil. And my readers may share the same curiosity. There is scarcely anything in my experience about which I could not give a more satisfactory answer. A new world had opened upon me. I lived more in one day than in a year of my slave life. It was a time of joyous excitement which words can but tamely describe. In a letter written to a friend soon after reaching New York, I said: "I felt as one might feel upon escape from a den of hungry lions." Anguish and grief, like darkness and rain, may be depicted; but gladness and joy, like the rainbow, defy the skill of pen or pencil.[6]

In *My Bondage and My Freedom* (1855), Douglass describes his visit to Ireland, where relations between black and white people were much different from what he had experienced at home:

I breathe, and lo! the slave becomes a man. I gaze around in vain for one who will question my equal humanity, claim me as his slave, or offer me an insult. I employ a cab—I am seated beside white people—I reach the hotel—I enter the same door—I am shown into the same parlor—I dine at the same table—and no one is offended. . . . I find myself regarded and treated at every turn with the kindness and deference [respect] paid to white people. When I go to church, I am met by no upturned nose and scornful lip.[7]

BIOGRAPHY

Frederick Douglass

1818–1895

BORN: Talbot County, Maryland

ROLE: Abolitionist, writer, public speaker, and politician

Frederick Douglass was born a slave. The wife of Douglass' owner taught Douglass the alphabet—an act that was illegal. When the slave owner found out, he was furious, as he believed that education would make slaves rebellious. But Douglass continued to teach himself to read and write, and he became very well educated.

Douglass escaped in 1838 and headed to the North, where he became a major speaker for the abolition movement. He also championed women's rights.

ATTEMPTS AT COMPROMISE

Despite the many differences dividing North and South, in the first half of the 19th century politicians managed to make a series of **compromises** that kept the country intact. These compromises sometimes left decisions about difficult issues up to individual states, not the **federal** government. Other times, the federal government made decisions for states. This issue of states' rights (see box) divided the country in the years leading up to the war.

The Missouri Compromise of 1820 said that Missouri became a state with slaves. Territories north of the southern border of Missouri would be free, while territories to the south of that would decide for themselves whether they would be slave owning or free. Maine would be admitted to the Union as a free state.[8]

States' rights

The federal government of the United States deals with matters that affect the whole nation, such as relations with other countries. State governments deal with matters that are not the responsibility of the federal government. Laws in each state are often different from those of other states.

The U.S. Constitution addresses the issue of states' rights, thanks to the 10th **Amendment**, passed in 1791. This amendment says that any laws not reserved for, or prohibited (prevented) by, the federal government belong to the states or to the people. (However, when the Constitution was written in 1787, the issue of slavery was too difficult to resolve. The problem was left for future generations to solve.)

In the years leading up to the Civil War, many southerners believed that it was very important that each state should decide how it was run—for example, that a state with an economy tied to slavery should be allowed to support slavery. Many southerners saw federal moves to get rid of slavery as an attack on southern civilization. Their economy depended on slaves to work the plantations.

THE COMPROMISE OF 1850

Then in 1850, Congress passed another compromise. This agreed, among other things, that California would join the Union as a free state, even though half of it was below the line of the Missouri Compromise. But as part of this compromise, slavery was still allowed in the capital city, Washington—but the slave trade was banned. This angered the South.[9]

According to the Compromise of 1850, there would also be a strengthened Fugitive Slave Act. This law said that slave catchers from the South were allowed to enter northern free states to arrest escaped slaves and force them back to the South. Northern lawmen were required to assist them or face large fines. Abolitionists were outraged. This compromise pushed the different views of slavery to the breaking point.

Uncle Tom's Cabin

In 1852 *Uncle Tom's Cabin,* written by the prominent abolitionist Harriet Beecher Stowe, was published. The story was about the cruelty of a white southern slave owner, who eventually murders his elderly and saint-like slave, Tom. The book had a huge impact on opinions in the North at a moment when tensions were already on the rise. When Stowe met President Abraham Lincoln in 1862, Lincoln is alleged to have greeted her by saying, "So you are the little woman who wrote the book that started this great war."[10]

Henry Clay (center) gives a speech on the Compromise of 1850 to the Senate.

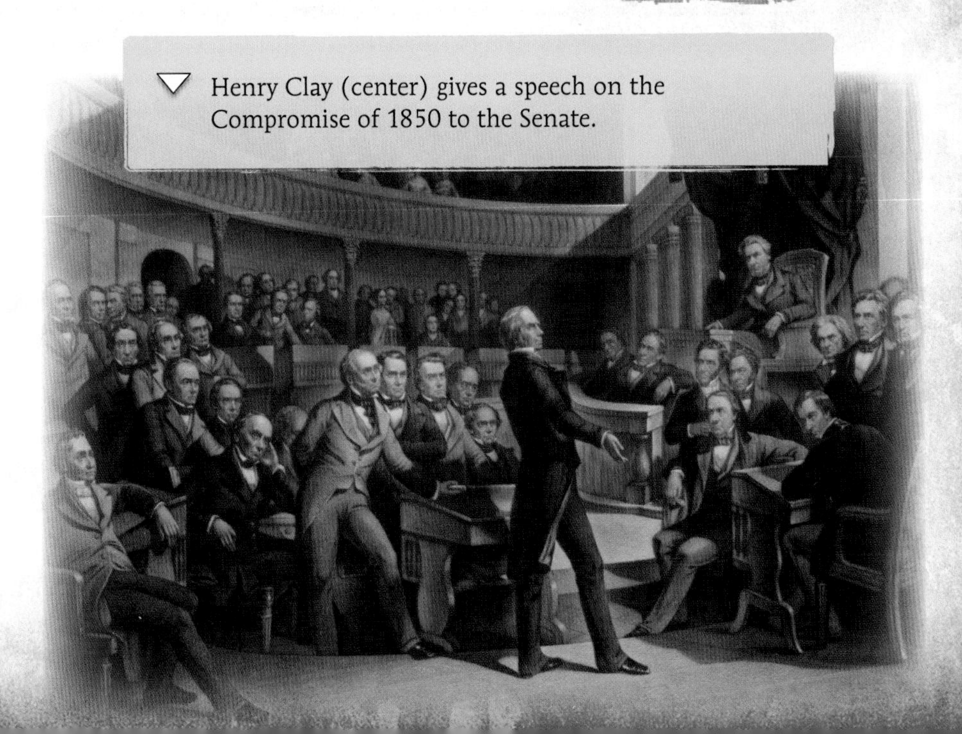

"BLEEDING KANSAS"

In 1854 the Kansas-Nebraska Act organized the territories of Kansas and Nebraska. The two territories were then allowed to decide for themselves whether they would permit slavery. Congress assumed that Nebraska would be a free state, while the people of Kansas would vote for slavery if they wanted it.[11]

But Kansas proved to be a problem. Abolitionists persuaded many antislavery farmers to move there—and eventually cast votes against slavery in the state. In response, proslavery southerners who called themselves "border ruffians" went from Missouri to Kansas in March 1855 to increase the number of votes for slavery, sometimes by voting several times.[12]

In May 1856 some "ruffians" attacked an abolitionist settlement. To retaliate, abolitionists, led by the antislavery fanatic John Brown, murdered five men. The violence was carried on for four months, with smaller events occurring for several years. The state became known as "Bleeding Kansas." About 55 people died as a result of the struggle over slavery there. This tragedy increased the passions of many opponents of slavery in the North.

POLITICAL PARTIES

For the first decades after U.S. independence, politicians and presidents acted as individuals. Political parties did not come in until the presidency of Andrew Jackson between 1829 and 1837. Jackson led the Democrats, and they made changes that gave greater power to the president. The National Republicans didn't agree with this—they were joined by some southern Democrats. Around 1834 they began calling themselves Whigs. Whigs believed in national projects such as roads and railways, whereas the Democrats were more interested in the powers of individual states.

When slavery became a major division in the country, a new party opposing slavery was formed in 1854, the Republicans. They quickly became very popular, and the Whigs faded away, putting up their last presidential candidate in 1856. In 1857 the Dred Scott court case ended with a pro-slavery judge ruling that no African American was, nor could ever be, a U.S. citizen. The judge also said that the Missouri Compromise was unconstitutional. The Southern states were pleased, but the North was outraged.

In June 1858 Abraham Lincoln was made the Illinois Republican candidate for the Senate. He made a speech known as "A House Divided." In it, Lincoln stated that a house divided against itself cannot stand, meaning that a country which is half slave owning and half free cannot survive. The continuation of the Union was essential to him. Later that year Lincoln had seven debates with his Democratic Party rival Stephen A. Douglas. They argued about slavery and popular sovereignty, part of states' rights. At the time Lincoln was little known but the debate drew the attention of the whole nation. Douglas was elected.

The year 1859 saw the debate over slavery and states' rights continue. John Brown's raid stirred things up even more. Lincoln made more speeches. In 1860 Jefferson Davis made resolutions in the Senate supporting slavery. When Lincoln was elected as the Republican presidential candidate in 1860 war was brought nearer as the South saw him as their greatest foe.

BIOGRAPHY

Abraham Lincoln 1809–1865

BORN: Hardin County, Kentucky

ROLE: President of the United States from 1861 to 1865

Abraham Lincoln was a lawyer and impressive speaker. He sat in the Illinois state legislature from 1834 to 1842 and was elected to congress in 1846. In 1856 he joined the Republican Party, and in 1860 he won the party's nomination for president.

Lincoln made the Republican Party a powerful organization and persuaded the Democrats in the North to support the Union. He always said that the preservation of the Union was his main motive for the war. In an effort to win the war, Lincoln assumed more power than any president before him, declaring martial law and suspending legal rights.[13]

SECESSION AND THE BATTLE OF FORT SUMTER

After Abraham Lincoln was elected president in the fall of 1860, the conflicts dividing the United States reached a boiling point. For many, compromise was no longer an option.

On December 20, 1860, South Carolina became the first state to secede from the United States. In January and February 1861, six other southern states also seceded—Mississippi, Florida, Alabama, Georgia, Louisiana, and Texas.

In early February, Alabama invited the other secessionist states to meet in Montgomery to form a new government, called the Confederate States of America. Representatives there formed a new constitution and elected Jefferson Davis as the Confederacy's first president.

Capital cities

Both the Union and the Confederacy established capital cities during the Civil War. The Union retained Washington, D.C., the U.S. capital that was specially created as the national capital after the Revolutionary War. The Confederacy chose Montgomery, Alabama, at the beginning of the war, but it proved too small. So, Richmond, Virginia, was named as the new Confederate capital at the end of May 1861. After the Union Army captured Richmond in 1865, Danville, Virginia, became the capital for the few last days of war.

BIOGRAPHY

Jefferson Davis 1808–1889

BORN: Christian County, Kentucky

ROLE: President of the Confederate States of America from 1861 to 1865

Jefferson Davis trained as a military officer. He later became a senator in the House of Representatives. He was U.S. secretary for war in 1853. Davis was against secession but loyal to his state. He made a farewell speech to the Senate in Washington saying Northern senators were not his enemies. His home state of Mississippi made him leader of their forces.[1] Then he was called to be president of the Confederacy. After the Civil War he was imprisoned for two years and indicted for **treason**.

THE BATTLE OF FORT SUMTER, APRIL 1861

South Carolina's capital, Charleston, had a harbor guarded by Fort Sumter. There was a federal **garrison** there. Since South Carolina no longer considered it part of the federal government, local troops wanted to drive these federal troops out. So, they attacked the fort on April 12–13, 1861. About 85 federal soldiers were suddenly faced with about 500 Confederate troops.[2]

A Union ship tried to take supplies to the garrison, but it was driven off by Confederate **artillery**. For two days, southern guns pounded the fort. Short of men, ammunition, and food, the northern commander, Major Robert Anderson, agreed to evacuate the fort. No one was killed in the battle, but two federal soldiers died when their cannon exploded during the ceremony of surrender.

People on both sides realized that this was a very important event. It led to calls for more military action from both northerners and southerners. President Lincoln, who had just become president on March 4, called for 75,000 volunteers for the new Union Army, to stop the rebellion. In part in reaction to this, four more southern states seceded—Virginia, Arkansas, North Carolina, and Tennessee.

THE DEFENSE OF FORT SUMTER

Here is what Major Robert Anderson, the commanding officer representing the federal government, wrote in his report about what happened at Fort Sumter. He is also explaining why he surrendered, just in case he was put on trial for giving up his post. (Note: The language of this, and some other excerpts in this book, has been edited in places to be more understandable by a modern student reader.)

New York, April 19, 1861.

Colonel,
I have the honor to send herewith dispatches Nos. 99 and 100, written at but not mailed in Fort Sumter, and to state that I shall, at as early a date as possible, forward a detailed report of the operations in the harbor of Charleston, S.C., in which my command bore a part on the 12th and 13th, ending with the evacuation of Fort Sumter, and the withdrawal, with the honors of war, of my garrison on the 14th from that harbor, after having sustained for thirty-four hours the fire from seventeen 10-inch ***mortars*** *and from batteries of heavy guns, well placed and well served, by the forces under the command of Brigadier-General Beauregard. Fort Sumter is left in ruins from the effect of the* ***shell*** *and shot from his batteries, and officers of his army reported that our firing had destroyed most of the buildings inside Fort Moultrie. God was pleased to guard my little force from the shell and shot which were thrown into and against my work, and to Him are our thanks due that I am enabled to report that no one was seriously injured by their fire. I regret that I have to add that, in consequence of some unaccountable misfortune, one man was killed, two seriously and three slightly wounded whilst saluting our flag as it was lowered.*

I have the honor to be, very respectfully, your obedient servant,
Robert Anderson,
Major, First Regiment Artillery, &c.[3]

Confederate eyewitness General. S. W. Crawford describes the condition of Sumter when Anderson agreed to its surrender:

"It was a scene of ruin and destruction. The quarters and barracks were in ruins. The main gates and the planking of the windows were gone. The weapons stores closed and surrounded by smouldering flames and burning ashes. Food had run out and there were only four barrels of gunpowder available. The effect of the direct shot had been to batter the walls, where the marks could be counted by hundreds, while the shells, in connection with hot shot, which set them on fire, had destroyed the barracks and quarters down to the gun casemates, while the gunfire from the side had prevented the service of the barbette guns, some of them comprising the most important battery in the work. The breaching fire from the columbiads (type of big cannon) and the rifle gun at Cummings point must have eventually succeeded if continued, but as yet no guns had been disabled or injured at that point. The effect of the fire upon the parapet was clear. The right face, as well as the left face, were all taken in reverse, and a destructive fire maintained until the end, while the gun carriages were destroyed in the fire of the blazing quarters."[4]

This photo shows the wreckage of Fort Sumter after it surrendered in 1861. The Confederate flag is flying on the flagpole.

THE VIEW FROM WASHINGTON, D.C., APRIL 1861

These are extracts from the diary of Horatio Nelson Taft, who lived in Washington, D.C. He was employed in the U.S. Patents Office, specializing in **armaments**. Taft's family was friendly with President Lincoln's, and their children played together. Taft witnessed events and people's feelings as the war started, and his diary serves as a very useful tool to understand what it was like in Washington, D.C., at the time.

The diary is in the Library of Congress. It was kept private by the Taft family until 2000. The sometimes-odd spellings of words are just as Taft wrote them.

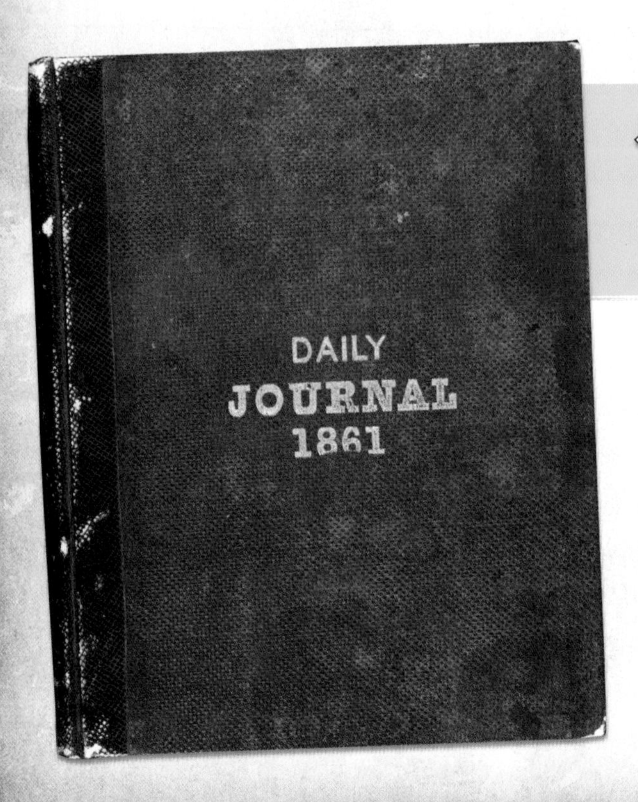

This photograph shows the actual journal of Horatio Nelson Taft.

TUESDAY 9
Much anxiety is felt on account of the fleet which for two or three days past has been leaving NY with troops &c for the South. Many are fearing an attack upon the City now, as it is thought that a War is about commencing.

WEDNESDAY, APRIL 10, 1861
The District Militia were all out on parade and eight Companies entered the service of the U.S. upon requisition of the Secretary of War for the Protection of the City. The guards are doubled at all the Public Buildings, and Military companies were on duty all last night. Exciting rumors from the South & exciting news expected.

THURSDAY 11
City full of Military and full of excitement. Nothing heard from Charleston unusual, but news expected by tomorrow. Fort Sumpter, it is now thought, is without doubt to be relieved in some way. The Cotton States are all up in Arms.

FRIDAY 12
Went with Juliet and the boys to see the soldiers over to the Long Bridge. Nothing but the guard there. Visited the City Armory, a company of U.S. Artillery stationed there. The Military companies are now divided and stationed at various points all over the City. Treason is in our midst. One hardly knows whom to trust. But I speak my own sentiments freely as I have all the time and denounce "seceders" as Traitors. Went down to the Ave & got the NY papers. It is said today that Fort Sumpter has been provisioned without bloodshed.

SATURDAY, APRIL 13, 1861
This has been the most exciting day yet. The last report about the provisioning Ft Sumpter was untrue and today or early this morning news came that the Rebels were bombarding it and tonight the report is that Maj Anderson has surrendered, it being on fire. The last report is not generaly credited. Even if true, it is not astonishing. The Rebels have ten thousand men & nineteen Batteries. Anderson had 70 men only.

SUNDAY 14
The excitement in the City increases all the time now the war has begun. But the reports from Charleston are mostly "bogus." Maj Anderson has probably not surrendered, but there is fighting there. I left Willards about 1/2 past 10 this evening, never saw a more excited crowd. The President has made requisition upon the States for 75,000 men or Volunteers to defend the Government. Think of sending my family out of the City immediately.

MONDAY 15
It seems pretty probable that "Sumpter" is taken but I think that we cannot rely entirely upon the news. There seems to be a great war spirit up throughout the Country. Washington will soon be a great Military Camp. My wife is not so much frightened today. I think we will not hurry in getting the family off.[5]

A NATION AT WAR

There would be over 1,000 battles between the beginning and end of the Civil War. Some were almost-bloodless skirmishes, while others were huge battles involving tens of thousands of soldiers and lasting several days. Most battles took place in the southeastern parts of the United States. However, there were actions as far south as Texas and in western areas such as New Mexico and Arizona. The biggest battle of the war was fought the farthest north, in Gettysburg, Pennsylvania.

FIRST BATTLE OF BULL RUN (BATTLE OF MANASSAS), JULY 1861

After the attack on Fort Sumter, northern newspapers demanded that President Lincoln begin an attack on the South. But this was before Union troops were properly trained. Union General Irvin McDowell was told to advance on Confederate troops led by General P. Beauregard, who were stationed at Manassas Junction, Virginia.[1]

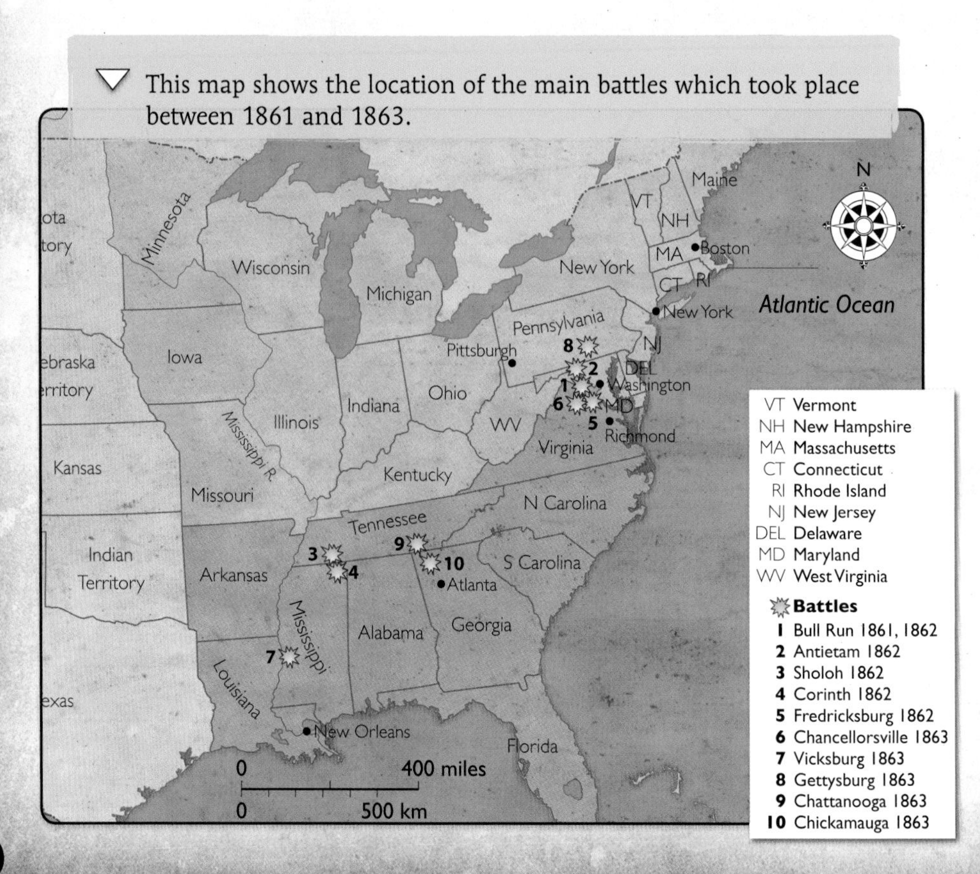

This map shows the location of the main battles which took place between 1861 and 1863.

McDowell attacked on July 21, 1861, and he was initially successful. But the introduction of Confederate reinforcements resulted in a Confederate victory. Union troops began a chaotic retreat toward Washington, D.C.

BATTLE OF SHILOH, APRIL 1862

Over 100,000 soldiers were involved in the Battle of Shiloh, in southwestern Tennessee. Union soldiers under General Ulysses S. Grant (see box) had penetrated deep into Tennessee, traveling by river. On April 6, 1862, the Confederates, led by General Albert Johnston and General Beauregard, decided to launch a surprise attack to split the Union forces. Their attack was helped by the fact that Grant did not dig defenses around his camp.

The Confederates almost broke through, but the Union Army defended desperately. The next day Grant was reinforced by the Army of the Ohio and began a counterattack. The Confederates were forced to retreat. This was the bloodiest battle of the war so far, with Union **casualties** numbering over 13,000, and Confederate losses reaching nearly 11,000—including General Johnston, who was killed on the first day. Both sides were shocked, suddenly realizing that the war would not be won by a single large battle.

BIOGRAPHY

Ulysses S. Grant 1822–1885

BORN: Point Pleasant, Ohio

ROLE: Military hero, Union military leader, and U.S. president

Ulysses S. Grant became a soldier at the West Point Military Academy in 1839. He fought in the Mexican-American War. He resigned from the U.S. Army in 1854, but he went on to offer his services to the Union Army in 1861.

Grant was promoted to major-general after several victories on the Mississippi and given command of the Army of the Tennessee. Heavy losses were typical of Grant's battles. After important victories, he was put in charge of the entire Union Army in March 1864. He planned the strategy that led to the Confederacy's final defeat. In 1868 Grant was elected president of the United States. He served two terms.[2]

THE ARMIES

Both sides in the Civil War formed substantial armed forces from very early in the war. The armed forces were organized, in theory, in this way:

1) *Armies*: Armies were the largest of the military units. The Union armies tended to be named after rivers—for example, the Army of the Mississippi. The Confederate armies tended to be named after states or regions—for example, the Army of Missouri. There were at least 16 armies on the Union side and 23 on the Confederate side.
2) *Corps*: **Corps** were composed of two or more divisions and, except for the **cavalry** corps, they included all arms of service, such as **infantry** and artillery.[3] Union corps were given a Roman number (for example, "XV"). Confederate corps also had numbers, but they were often named after their commander—for example, Jackson's Corps.
3) *Divisions*: Divisions were made of a number of **brigades** (see below). They were supposed to have about 12,000 soldiers, but in reality, due to losses and illness, there were only about half that number or less.
4) *Brigades*: The tactical infantry unit of the Civil War, the brigade generally consisted of four to six **regiments**.
5) *Infantry regiments*: Infantry regiments were generally composed of 10 companies. In the Union Army, an infantry company had a maximum authorized strength of 101 officers and men, and a minimum strength of 83.

THE SOLDIERS

Most soldiers were in the infantry. These were foot soldiers who marched to move from one place to another. In infantry battles, two lines of soldiers would line up on opposite sides, standing up and firing their guns at each other at close range. This continued until one side—because of losses or fear—broke and retreated.

Cavalry soldiers used swords, carbines (short-barreled rifles), and pistols. Soldiers who worked big guns like cannons were the artillery. Field artillery could be moved around on wheels by teams of horses or mules and be used on battlefields. Static artillery, using huge guns, was used in both attack and defense during sieges and bombardments.

A group of Union soldiers sit on a hill overlooking Cumberland Landing. The landing was used as a staging area by the Army of the Potomac in 1862.

New ways of moving soldiers were developed during the Civil War, as groups of soldiers traveled by riverboats and by railroad. This sped up movement and could lead to surprise attacks or last-minute reinforcements for the defense.

THE WEAPONS

Developments in weapons made the Civil War very lethal and bloody. Infantry soldiers' guns were loaded from the front, although some repeating rifles were in use. They were called **Minié rifles.**[4] The standard make was the Sharps rifle. Whereas the **muskets** of previous times were inaccurate and short range, the Sharps had twice the range and were accurate. Rifles were fitted with **bayonets** so that infantrymen could stab each other at very close quarters.

Artillery guns, which could fire much greater distances than infantry rifles, were mostly loaded from the front. There were many different types. The big difference from earlier times was that their barrels were rifled. That means that they had spiral grooves inside the barrel, which made the solid shot or explosive shell spin. It could go further and also be more accurate and destructive.

SECOND BATTLE OF BULL RUN (SECOND BATTLE OF MANASSAS), AUGUST 1862

In August 1862, in Virginia, Confederate General Thomas Jonathan "Stonewall" Jackson ordered an attack on a Union column that was passing across his front. The fighting lasted several hours, but it was not decisive.

Union General John Pope then became convinced that he had trapped Jackson, so he concentrated the bulk of his army against him. On August 29, Pope launched a series of assaults against Jackson's position along an unfinished railroad track. The attacks were repulsed, with heavy casualties on both sides. When Confederate artillery devastated a Union assault, 28,000 Confederates counterattacked, in what would be the largest mass assault of the war. The left side of the Union Army was crushed, and the Union forces were driven back to Bull Run.[5] Only an effective Union **rear guard** action prevented a repeat of the First Bull Run disaster (see page 22).

BATTLE OF ANTIETAM, SEPTEMBER 1862

In September 1862, Confederate General Robert E. Lee saw the opportunity to invade Maryland. Union General George B. McClellan was sent to stop him. The two armies met at Antietam Creek, near

A painting of the 1862 Battle of Antietam. Union forces have blue uniforms and Confederates are in gray. This image is exaggerated and romanticized.

Sharpsburg, Maryland. Lee was outnumbered by almost two to one, but he was able to stop the Union Army units from joining up into a powerful mass. The battle raged back and forth all day on September 17, but neither side was able to gain a decisive advantage.

The losses on both sides were enormous, as this was the bloodiest single-day battle of the Civil War. Union casualties were over 12,000, and Confederate losses were just over 10,000 men. By nightfall both sides were exhausted. Lee went back to Virginia, and McClellan did nothing to stop him.[6]

△ Unlike the painting on page 26, this image shows the reality of the Battle of Antietam. Dead Confederate soldiers lie in a shallow ditch, looked at by Union soldiers.

The Emancipation Proclamation

The Battle of Antietam had no decisive winner, but President Lincoln claimed a victory for the Union. This victory allowed him to issue the Emancipation Proclamation on January 1, 1863. This order said that all slaves in the Confederate states were now free. In southern areas that were occupied by the Union Army, the slaves were immediately freed. Freed slaves joined the Union Army in large numbers.

The Emancipation Proclamation had several important effects. From this point onward, slavery and abolition became central to the North's war aims. The proclamation inspired the northern antislavery movement to pursue the war until its end. It also changed the opinion of European nations that had been sympathetic to the Confederacy. Now that slavery was clearly a major issue at stake, these countries withdrew their support for the South. Northern Democrats suddenly had problems because of the proclamation, however. They had tended to support southern views on slavery.[7]

BATTLE OF FREDERICKSBURG, DECEMBER 1862

General McClellan was fairly unsuccessful, so President Lincoln replaced him with General Ambrose E. Burnside. Burnside decided to attack Richmond, Virginia, via the important Virginia town of Fredericksburg.

Although the Union Army was 115,000 strong and the Confederate defenders had only a few thousand men, Burnside hesitated for three weeks before attacking. This gave General Lee (see box) time to dig defenses on the other side of the town. When Burnside did attack, beginning on December 13, it was a disaster.

BIOGRAPHY

Robert E. Lee 1807–1870

BORN: Stratford Hall, Virginia

ROLE: General in charge of the Confederate Army at the end of the war; the most famous Confederate general of the Civil War

Robert E. Lee came from a famous military family. He was a top student at the West Point Military Academy. He was an officer in the U.S. Army for 36 years before the Civil War started. Lee was against slavery and **secession**, but because he came from Virginia, he joined the Confederate cause.

Because of Lee's brilliant military thinking, he was able to defeat larger and better-equipped Union forces on many occasions. However, he suffered a major defeat at the Battle of Gettysburg. He finally had to surrender at Appomattox in 1865. Lee was idolized by his soldiers and the people of the South. He also gained the respect of people in the North.[8]

DID YOU KNOW? Lee led the troops who captured John Brown at Harper's Ferry. In early 1861 President Lincoln offered command of all Union troops to Lee. He turned it down to return to Virginia. His U.S. citizenship was restored in 1975, 105 years after his death.

"This is a terrible war coming, and these young men who have never seen war cannot wait for it to happen, but I tell you, I wish that I owned every slave in the South, for I would free them all to avoid this war." Robert E. Lee

The Union Army took huge losses, while the Confederates' casualties were light. The North was demoralized by this pointless battle, and Burnside was fired. This battle marked a high point of Confederate fortunes, leading Lee to decide to invade the North.

BATTLE OF CHANCELLORSVILLE, APRIL–MAY 1863

The Battle of Chancellorsville was fought in Virginia from May 1 to May 5, 1863. It was regarded as General Lee's finest victory. He defeated the Union Army, which was led by General Joseph Hooker, and stopped the Union advance to the South.

However, this success was clouded by the death of General "Stonewall" Jackson (see box), whom Lee called his "right arm." Jackson was wounded during a confused nighttime **reconnaissance** mission.

BIOGRAPHY

Thomas Jonathan "Stonewall" Jackson

1824–1863

BORN: Clarksburg, Virginia

ROLE: Successful Confederate general

Before the war, "Stonewall" Jackson was a professor at the Virginia Military Institute. Jackson showed great skill at the two battles of Bull Run (1861 and 1862), Harpers Ferry (1862), Antietam (1862), Fredericksburg, and Chancellorsville. He also captured the Union supply center at Manassas Junction, Virginia. At Chancellorsville, he was returning in the darkness to his headquarters when he was accidentally fired at by some Confederate troops. He was wounded and had to have his left arm **amputated**. Eight days later he died of pneumonia.[9]

WHAT WAS IT LIKE TO BE A SOLDIER?

Like soldiers in all wars, life for Civil War soldiers was filled mainly with boredom, dirt, bad food like salt pork and hardtack (a kind of rock-hard biscuit), disease, and training. The fear and excitement of action in battle was occasional.

Soldiers wrote the passages here, which show some of the things they experienced. These two extracts clearly show the difference between the everyday boredom of life in a military camp and the experience of being in action.

This shows a heavy artillery gun in action. The soldier in the foreground is pulling on a rope that will make the gun fire.

A CONFEDERATE SOLDIER'S MEMOIR

The following is part of a letter from Absolom A. Harrison, of the 4th Regiment, Kentucky Cavalry Volunteers, written on January 19, 1862:

There is a good many of our men sick for we have been laying on the wet ground ever since we have been here without any straw under us. And the water runs under us every time it rains. There is only about two thirds of the men fit for duty at this time. Our camp was very nice when we first came here. But it is knee deep in mud now. We don't get more than half enough to eat and our horses are not half fed. We get up at 6 o'clock and answer roll call. Then we feed and brush our horses and wash which takes up the time till 7 when we eat our breakfast. Then we water our horses. Then drill on foot until dinner. Then at 1-1/2 o'clock we go out and drill on horseback until 4. Then water, feed and brush our horses. Then get wood for the night. By this time it is after dark. So you see they keep us pretty busy.[10]

A UNION SOLDIER'S MEMOIR

The following passage is from the 1863 "Vicksburg Diary" of R. W. Burt, a lieutenant in the 76th Ohio Infantry:

Week after week we remained on this hill, occasionally seeing the rebels raising their heads above their works across the deep hollow between us and them, and shots were frequently exchanged. We had to keep very close under the shelter of our rifle pits made for our protection, for whenever we exposed ourselves to the view of the enemy we were sure to draw their fire. One day I was walking along the summit of the hill when a Minié ball struck the ground only a few feet before me, raising the dust and causing me to seek a safer location before another shot should follow, perhaps more to my discomfort.[11]

THE TIDE TURNS: VICTORY FOR THE UNION

Beginning in the summer of 1863, a series of battles turned the tide of the war toward a Union victory.

THE SIEGE OF VICKSBURG, MAY–JULY 1863

Vicksburg, in Mississippi, was a very important city. It controlled the Mississippi River, the major thoroughfare from the North to the South. General Grant and General William T. Sherman fought a series of battles from 1862 to try to gain control of Vicksburg.

In mid-May, Confederate soldiers under General John C. Pemberton became separated from other Confederate forces. Pemberton retreated to Vicksburg, which had miles of very strong defenses.

On May 22, 1863, General Grant started a long siege on Vicksburg, using artillery and gunboats to bombard the city. Civilians hid in caves, and the Confederate soldiers were weakened by disease and starvation. In this campaign, General Grant demonstrated the skill and determination that marked him as the most successful Union general. On July 4, 1863, the siege ended when Pemberton surrendered. The Union now controlled the all-important Mississippi River, a fact that continued until the end of the war.[1]

THE BATTLE OF GETTYSBURG, JULY 1863

The Battle of Gettysburg was the most important battle in the Civil War. It had the highest casualty count of any battle and marked a political turning point.

Following his victory at Chancellorsville in May 1863, General Lee received approval from the Confederate government to invade the North. Lee's army moved unchecked into Pennsylvania. At this point, the Union had replaced General Hooker with General George Gordon

Meade. Lee decided to bring his entire army east of the mountains and prepare for battle. At the same time, Meade moved his army north. By June 30, both armies were converging upon Gettysburg, Pennsylvania, and a major battle was set to begin.

The battle began at 5:30 a.m. on July 1, 1863. Soon after 10:30 a.m., Union troops arrived and engaged Confederate General Henry Heth along McPherson's Ridge. By 11:30 a.m., Heth's forces had been defeated. Lee arrived on the battlefield after noon. He had hoped to avoid a general battle, since the strength of the enemy was unknown and the Gettysburg area was unfamiliar. The day's fighting had resulted in a Confederate victory, but Union forces held onto the high ground south of Gettysburg, where their position was soon strengthened by reinforcements.

Encouraged by the success of his army in the fighting on July 1, Lee decided to renew the battle on July 2. But this time the Union Army was well prepared for Lee's offensive. The second day of fighting cost each army some 9,000 casualties. Lee's forces had again gained ground, but they failed to dislodge the Union Army from its strong position. General Meade decided to hold his position.[2]

Confederates charge up Little Round Top, held by the 20th Maine Regiment. This was an incident in the Battle of Gettysburg.

THE GETTYSBURG ADDRESS

The site of the Battle of Gettysburg was later made into a cemetery. On November 19, 1863, President Lincoln made a speech at the opening of the cemetery. This speech, known as the Gettysburg Address, is considered to be one of the most important political speeches in U.S. history. It is sometimes called the "Second Declaration of Independence."

Lincoln was known as a great speaker, and he used this gift throughout his career to inspire people. Now, with the Gettysburg Address, his words were encouraging the North in its mission. Although Lincoln initially thought that he had not done very well, this very short speech inspired the Union toward victory.

This photograph by Mathew Brady shows President Lincoln (bare-headed and in the center of the crowd) making the Gettysburg Address in 1863.

The content of the Gettysburg Address is as follows:

*Four **score** and seven years ago our fathers brought forth on this continent, a new nation, conceived in Liberty, and dedicated to the proposition that all men are created equal. Now we are engaged in a great civil war, testing whether that nation, or any nation so conceived and so dedicated, can long endure. We are met on a great battlefield of that war. We have come to dedicate a portion of that field, as a final resting place for those who here gave their lives that that nation might live. It is altogether fitting and proper that we should do this. But, in a larger sense, we cannot dedicate—we cannot **consecrate**—we cannot **hallow**—this ground. The brave men, living and dead, who struggled here, have consecrated it, far above our poor power to add or detract. The world will little note, nor long remember what we say here, but it can never forget what they did here. It is for us the living, rather, to be dedicated here to the unfinished work which they who fought here have thus far so nobly advanced. It is rather for us to be here dedicated to the great task remaining before us—that from these honored dead we take increased devotion to that cause for which they gave the last full measure of devotion—that we here highly resolve that these dead shall not have died in vain—that this nation, under God, shall have a new birth of freedom—and that government of the people, by the people, for the people, shall not perish from the earth.*[3]

President Lincoln was reminding people of the revolution that created the United States. He was saying that the people who died in the battle made the ultimate sacrifice to preserve the union. He said it was left up to soldiers of his day to ensure that the United States continued to be united under the democratic principles on which it was founded. Unlike the Confederates, President Lincoln believed that the equality that he was talking about meant equality for all, including African Americans.

CHICKAMAUGA, SEPTEMBER 1863

Chattanooga was a major communications center in Tennessee. The Union Army drove the Confederates out of the area. But General Braxton Bragg, the Confederate commander, was determined to get the town back.

On September 19 and 20, 1863, the two armies met at a creek called Chickamauga, in nearby Georgia. Fighting in dense woodland led to some chaos. After two days of fighting, the Union troops pulled back to Chattanooga, while the Confederates occupied the hills around it. The battle is considered a Confederate victory. It cost over 34,000 casualties in total because of the chaos, becoming the second bloodiest battle of the war—after Gettysburg.[4]

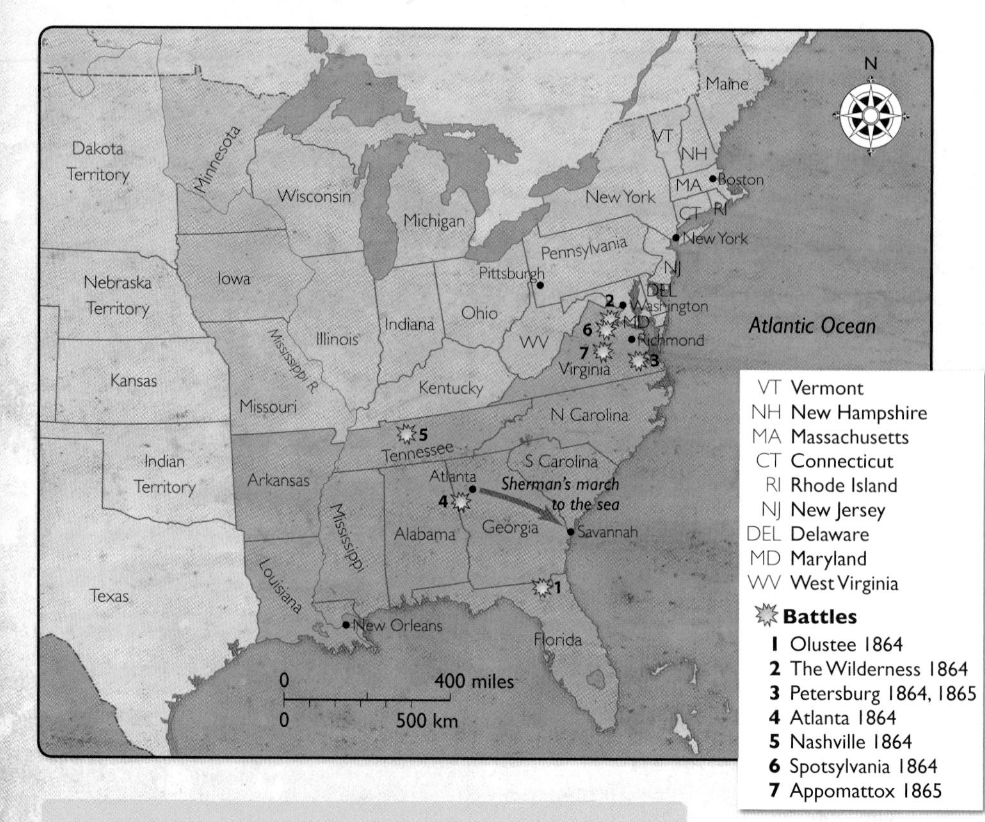

△ This map shows the location of the main battles from 1864 to 1865.

THE BATTLE OF THE WILDERNESS, MAY 1864

General Grant wanted to fight the Confederates' Army of Northern Virginia. The first clash was at the Wilderness, in Virginia, from May 5 to May 7, 1864. Fighting was fierce but inconclusive, as both sides attempted to maneuver in the dense woods. Darkness halted the fighting, and both sides rushed reinforcements forward. At 11:00 a.m. on May 6, a devastating Confederate **flank attack** died out when General James Longstreet was wounded by his own men. The battle was a **draw**. However, unlike other Union generals, Grant did not retreat.[5]

THE BATTLE OF SPOTSYLVANIA COURT HOUSE, MAY 1864

As soon as the Battle of the Wilderness ended, General Grant sent his army to go to the Spotsylvania Court House, also in Virginia. Unknown to him, the Confederates were also marching there. On May 8, 1864, the Battle of Spotsylvania Court House started. It was to last 1½ weeks, after which both armies marched away on May 20.

There was very fierce hand-to-hand fighting. The Union suffered more casualties than the Confederates. One of them was the Union General John Sedgwick, who taunted infantrymen trying to dodge the rifle balls whistling past, saying that the Confederates "couldn't hit an elephant at this distance." Shortly after, Sedgwick was hit in the face and killed.

THE ATLANTA CAMPAIGN, MAY–SEPTEMBER 1864

During this same period, Atlanta, Georgia, became the center of fierce fighting. Atlanta was an important supply, manufacturing, and communications center. General Sherman advanced toward the city, under orders to destroy as many Confederate war supplies as possible. The campaign lasted from May 1 to September 8. It was made up of many small fights and skirmishes and a few big battles at Resaca, Peach Tree Creek, Atlanta, and Jonesboro.

After a siege by the Union Army on September 1, the Confederates, under General Hood, left Atlanta. Sherman's troops occupied the city. The civilians were evacuated. Sherman's army finally left in November, burning all but about 400 buildings in the city as part of Sherman's March to the Sea.[6]

MEMORIES OF THE BATTLE OF SPOTSYLVANIA COURT HOUSE

These are the memories of a Union soldier, George Norton Galloway, who was involved in the desperate fighting at Spotsylvania:

The Confederates for a few moments had the advantage of us, and made good use of their rifles. Our men went down by the score; the gallant Upton was the only mounted officer in sight. He bravely cheered his men, and begged them to "hold this point." All of his staff had been either killed, wounded, or dismounted. While the open ground in rear of the Confederate works was choked with troops, a section of Battery C, 5th United States Artillery, under Lieutenant Richard Metcalf, was brought into action and increased the carnage by opening at short range with double charges of canister. This staggered the enemy. These guns were only abandoned when all the drivers and gunners had been killed.

This is an imaginative print of the battle. Printmakers Currier and Ives made prints of many battles of the war. They were very popular at the time.

In this passage, the fact that all the staff officers serving Colonel Upton had been hit by enemy fire shows just how intense and close the fighting was. The cannons were also firing at point-blank range using canister shot. This is like a tube full of lead or steel balls, which spread out to kill lots of soldiers at the same time, like a giant shotgun cartridge.

Galloway went on to write:

Captain John D. Fish, of Upton's staff, who had until this time performed valuable service in conveying ammunition to the gunners, fell, pierced by a bullet. In a few moments the two brass guns of the 5th Artillery, cut and hacked by the bullets of both antagonists, lay unworked with their muzzles projecting over the enemy's works, and their wheels half sunk in the mud. Between the lines and near at hand lay the horses of these guns, completely riddled. The dead and wounded were torn to pieces by the canister as it swept the ground where they had fallen...

Hundreds of Confederates, dead or dying, lay piled over one another in those pits. The fallen lay three or four feet deep in some places, shot in and about the head. Rifles, equipment, ammunition, cannon, shot and shell, and broken foliage were strewn about. With much labour a detail of Union soldiers buried the dead by simply turning the captured breastworks [earth defenses] upon them. The ***trenches*** *were nearly full of muddy water. It was the most horrible sight I had ever witnessed.*

The slaughter was shocking, even to Galloway, who won a Medal of Honor for his bravery in the battle.

This is an official report on part of the battle by the Confederate officer Lieutenant General Richard C. Ewell:

"The enemy attacked in heavy force at earliest dawn, and though gallantly resisted, their numbers and the want of artillery enabled them to break through our lines, capturing Maj. Gen. Edward Johnson, Brig. Gen. G. H. Steuart, about 2,000 men, and 20 pieces of artillery. The smoke of the guns and the mist kept the air dark until a comparatively late hour, thereby assisting the enemy, as he was enabled to mass his troops as he chose. They poured through our lines in immense numbers, taking possession to the right and left of the Salient and keeping up a constant fire of artillery and musketry for twenty-four hours."[7]

SHERMAN'S MARCH TO THE SEA, NOVEMBER–DECEMBER 1864

On November 15, 1864, Union General Sherman led an army of 62,000 men in two groups, with 35,000 horses and 2,500 wagons, on an overland march to the important Confederate port of Savannah, on the coast of Georgia. He cut himself off from his supply lines, so his army had to live on what they could buy or steal. He wrote: "The utter destruction of roads, houses and people will cripple their [the Confederate's] military resources. . . . I can make Georgia howl!"

Both Lincoln and Grant were worried about the risks of this strategy, but they allowed Sherman to continue. Encountering little organized opposition, Sherman captured Savannah on December 21, 1864, and sent a letter to Lincoln saying the port was a Christmas present.

Sherman and his army later turned north for the Carolinas, using the same methods and covering 450 miles (724 kilometers) in 50 days. Sherman's army actually got bigger, as it was joined by freed slaves. The results of this march, together with Grant's victories in Virginia, destroyed the Confederacy's ability to continue the war. It is still argued whether the burning of Atlanta, the later burning of Columbia, South Carolina, and the **looting** by some Union troops were necessary, but there is no doubt that Sherman's march had a major effect on Southern morale and war fighting capability. Perhaps, even more important politically, the march made the North more willing to continue the war until victory was achieved.

THE SIEGE OF PETERSBURG, JUNE 1864–MARCH 1865

The Siege of Petersburg was really a series of battles around Petersburg, Virginia, fought from June 9, 1864, to March 25, 1865. It was not a classic military siege, in which a city is usually surrounded and all supply lines are cut off. Rather, the campaign was nine months of trench warfare in which Union forces (commanded by General Grant) assaulted Petersburg unsuccessfully. They then constructed trench lines that eventually extended over 30 miles (48 kilometers) from the eastern outskirts of Richmond, Virginia, to around the eastern and southern outskirts of Petersburg.

Petersburg was crucial to the supply of Confederate General Lee's army and the Confederate capital of Richmond. Numerous raids and battles were fought in attempts to cut off the railroad supply lines through Petersburg to Richmond. Lee finally abandoned both cities in April 1865. The Siege of Petersburg featured the Civil War's largest number of African American troops, who suffered heavy casualties.

THE APPOMATTOX CAMPAIGN, MARCH–APRIL 1865

In all the battles of the war, both sides had their successes and disasters. Eventually the industrial might, wealth, and superior numbers of the Union forces ground the Confederacy down.

The last campaign, called the Appomattox Campaign, was held on March 25 to April 9, 1865, in Virginia. At this battle, General Lee tried to break General Grant's stranglehold on Petersburg and Richmond. He failed. Lee could see that there was no more he could do, and he wanted to save lives. He asked Grant for terms of surrender at Appomattox.[8]

BIOGRAPHY

William Tecumseh Sherman 1820–1891

BORN: Lancaster, Ohio

ROLE: Union military leader

William Tecumseh Sherman studied at West Point Military Academy and served in the Mexican-American War. He left the U.S. Army in 1853, but failed in several jobs. In 1861 he volunteered for the Union Army. His career had its ups and downs, and one newspaper even claimed that he was insane.

Sherman formed a good relationship with General Grant. He led an attack on Atlanta. He then led the March to the Sea, leaving a trail of destruction. After capturing the port of Savannah, he marched north to help Grant attack Richmond. After the war Sherman became the commander of the U.S. Army until 1884. He has been called the first modern general.[9]

THE WAR AT SEA

The fighting between the Union and the Confederacy took place not only on land, but also on rivers and in the sea, mainly on the Atlantic coast and the Gulf of Mexico. On great rivers like the Mississippi, armies could move large numbers of troops by riverboat. Gunboats could also fire artillery to support troops on the land.

From the beginning of the war, President Lincoln saw that a **blockade** of Confederate ports would both stop them from receiving military supplies from abroad, and also prevent their exports from providing money to finance the war. At first most ships got through. But as the Union Navy got bigger, the South's trade was increasingly blocked. Union ships and forces eventually captured all the Confederate ports, including New Orleans, Louisiana; Mobile, Alabama; and Norfolk, Virginia.

"Damn the torpedoes, full speed ahead!"

David Farragut, a Union Navy commander, joined the navy when he was just nine years old. Years later, at the attack on Mobile, Alabama, in 1864, he is alleged to have had himself tied to his ship's mast to see above the smoke. When one of his ships hit a mine (then called torpedoes) and sank, he is said to have yelled, "Damn the torpedoes, full speed ahead!" This aggressive spirit has become a legend in the U.S. Navy—but no one is sure that he actually said this.[10]

CONFEDERATE COMMERCE RAIDERS

The Confederates tried to counter the Union's naval supremacy by using commerce raiders. These were ships that were used to capture or sink Union ships carrying supplies or goods to be sold. The Confederates' problem was that they did not have the shipyards to build commerce raiders. They did buy some from Britain, and the CSS *Alabama* was quite successful. Still, the commerce raiders did not have much influence on the result of the war.

THE BATTLE OF HAMPTON ROADS

A few years before the Civil War, both France and Britain had built new ships called **ironclads**. The wooden hulls of these ships were encased with iron armor. During the Civil War, both sides built ironclads like this. The Confederates converted the USS *Merrimack* into an ironclad and called it the CSS *Virginia*.

News of this ironclad reached the North. In response, the Union built the USS *Monitor*, which resembled an armored raft, with a deck only just above water level. What made the *Monitor* so revolutionary was that all of its firepower came from two 11-inch (28-centimeter) guns in a revolving **turret**.

In early 1862 the *Monitor* traveled from New York to Hampton Roads, an area near a harbor off Sewell's Point, Virginia. The *Virginia* and *Monitor* then engaged in the first duel between ironclad warships. The fighting on March 9 was a draw. Neither ironclad could inflict significant damage on the other.[12]

The CSS *Hunley*

The Confederate ship known as the CSS *Hunley* was made out of a metal tube designed by H. L. Hunley. It sank twice in trials, and Hunley himself was killed in a similar accident. Still, the *Hunley* did go to war and struck an explosive charge into the Union ship the USS *Housatonic*, outside Charleston Harbor in 1864. The Union ship sank, but so did the *Hunley*.[11]

A painting of the Battle of Hampton Roads.

PEOPLE IN THE CIVIL WAR

Many people were directly involved in the Civil War. Soldiers of course experienced the war itself, as well as the horrors of prison camps and poor medical treatment. Apart from soldiers, many other people had roles to play in the war. Spies—many of them women—disguised themselves as everyday citizens behind enemy lines. Countless doctors and nurses also worked on the front lines, trying to save lives.

A VARIETY OF CULTURES

People of diverse ethnic backgrounds and heritages were involved in the Civil War. Immigrants who had settled in the United States—from countries such as Germany, Sweden, Ireland, Britain, France, and Italy—volunteered or were drafted into the armies, mostly on the Union side. African Americans (both freedmen and former slaves) volunteered for the Union, especially after the Emancipation Proclamation (see page 27). Texans of Spanish descent fought on both sides. Two Union soldiers who won the Medal of Honor for bravery were Scottish American and Jewish American, respectively.

IRISH AMERICANS

In the late 19th century, there were many people of Irish descent in the United States. In the 1860 census (an official count of people), well over one and a half million Americans claimed to have been born in Ireland. The majority of these lived in the North, in cities such as Boston and New York. Irish people in the 19th century were often discriminated against because they were Catholic.

About 150,000 Irish Americans joined the Union Army. Most famous was the fabled Meagher's Irish Brigade, led by the showy Thomas Meagher. They went into battle with an emerald green flag with a large golden harp in its center, celebrating their heritage even in the midst of battle.

NATIVE AMERICANS

The majority of white Americans regarded Native Americans as foreigners. Nevertheless, just under 3,600 Native Americans served in the Union Army during the war. Perhaps the best-known Native American soldier was Colonel Ely Parker, who was present at Lee's surrender at Appomattox (see pages 60 and 61). General Stand Watie was a Cherokee leader who commanded a group of Cherokees fighting for the South. He was the last Confederate general to surrender in the war.[1]

A portrait of Brigadier General Stand Watie of the Confederate Army, who allied the Cherokee nation to the Confederate cause.

THE BRITISH

Great Britain was officially neutral throughout the Civil War, meaning it did not take a side. Britain was the world's leading industrial and economic power. It also had a very powerful navy. The Confederate plan to become a separate country was largely based on the hope that British and French forces would support the Confederate side, in order to continue receiving exports from the South such as cotton. But this did not happen—largely because this would have meant war with the Union, which neither Britain nor France wanted, especially because supporting the South would be supporting slavery after the Emancipation Proclamation.

Still, thousands of British people took part in the war. Antislavery supporters fought for the Union, while adventurers and supporters of the "underdogs" joined the Confederate Army. Some British women became nurses on both sides.[2]

SPIES

Spies were very active on both sides during the Civil War. Spying during the war was like a political chess game. Each side was fully aware of the existence of **counterintelligence** personnel. Yet each side was unable to defend against even the most basic spying. This was largely because, as they were all Americans, it was difficult to spot someone from the other side.

Getting to the other side's territory was relatively easy, since there was not one continuously manned border. Southerners could go north or to Europe and get information from politicians and soldiers. This was especially true of women spies—and there were many women spies.[3]

Nevertheless, the Confederate spy organization was rather chaotic. But the Union was more organized and led by Allan Pinkerton. Pinkerton later became famous for his detective agency, which fought some of the notorious criminals of the Old West. On the whole, the secrets of spying operations were kept very secret and were never revealed, even after the war.

OBSERVATION BALLOONS

Both sides used hot air balloons to look across the front line at their enemy's forces. Best known among the "aeronauts" was Thaddeus S. C. Lowe, who worked for the Union. He and others made numerous observations using hydrogen-filled balloons during the first two years of the war. At one time the Union Army had seven balloons in service.

Harriet Tubman: Spy

Harriet Tubman helped hundreds of slaves escape via the Underground Railroad. To help even more people escape slavery, Tubman decided to become a spy for the Union Army.

Tubman helped plan a raid to free slaves from plantations in South Carolina. On June 1, 1863, several hundred male Union soldiers—along with Tubman—set out on three gunboats early in the morning. The soldiers set fire to buildings and destroyed bridges, to interfere with the efforts of the Confederate Army. They also freed about 750 slaves. The Union forces did not lose one soldier in the attack. The Confederates offered a reward of $40,000 for Tubman, but she was never caught.[4]

Due to the lack of cooperation by the army, all ballooning ceased in 1863, thus depriving the Union of a useful military tool.

The Confederates also realized the value of aerial reconnaissance. It is often stated that the sole Confederate balloon was fabricated of silk from dresses donated by southern ladies. Actually, the South had at least three balloons in service, one made of cotton and two made from new bolts of silk of various colors. However, the Confederates' inability to produce the fuel hydrogen in the field forced them to abandon balloon operations in 1863.[5]

These men are working inside a Union military balloon, preparing it for observation action.

MEMORIES OF A WAR CAMP

PRISONER OF WAR CAMPS

At the very beginning of the war, there were no places to detain prisoners. So, both sides released them, on oath not to take up arms until they had been exchanged for an enemy captive of equal rank.

Later, prison camps developed on both sides. The most notorious camp was the Confederates' Andersonville prison camp, in Georgia. The North had its own bad prisons, such as Elmira, in New York. There would be over 400,000 prisoners of war during the Civil War.

Prisoner Sergeant C. N. Thorp, a Union soldier who was captured at the Battle of Chickamauga in 1863 (see page 36), described what Andersonville prison was like. The prisoners were left to fend for themselves in terrible conditions:

At the time we arrived in May 1864 I suppose there were about 15 to 18 acres enclosed by a huge fence. Outside the stockade, there were ladders erected leading to a platform about twelve or thirteen feet above the ground, on which the guards stood. The height of the platform would give the guard easy oversight of the interior of the prison and the top of the stockade made a good rest for his gun. Many of the guards lost no opportunity to shoot at a Yank [member of the Union]. There was a dead-line, formed by driving stakes into the ground. Beyond this line none dared to go unless he wished to commit suicide. There were thousands of men, many of them nearly naked, barefoot, black and filthy. The space inside was covered with rough shelters. Tents made by sewing two army blankets together and stretching them over a ridge-pole under which several men could crawl for shelter, to a little affair, made by stretching shirts, which could scarcely shelter two men.

We had now been in captivity about eight months and our clothing was in rags though we had been careful to keep it. During a heavy storm none of us could keep from getting soaked and those poor fellows who were without any shelter were much worse off than those who had only a blanket for a roof. Lack of vegetable food and lack of exercise led many of us to contract the dread disease, scurvy. The mouth would become infected, the gums swollen so the teeth could not be closed together and we would be unable to chew any solid food. The gums would become black and decayed and, in my own case, with long and sharp finger nails I could gouge away parts which were in such condition as to be exceedingly offensive to the smell.[6]

The poor conditions at Andersonville were really about mismanagement and shortages. But the commander, Captain Henry Wirz, was hanged for cruelty in November 1865.

A photograph of the Andersonville prison camp.

MEDICAL CARE

During the Civil War, a soldier's chances of not surviving the war were about one in four. This was in part because little was known about what caused disease, how to stop it from spreading, or how to cure it. It was also because a few poorly qualified and undersupplied medical workers treated the wounded. Many doctors had limited abilities to perform surgery. The most common operation was amputation, the cutting off of limbs.

Gradually, doctors increased in numbers and skills. Still, nearly all the doctors served as apprentices instead of studying. Even those who had attended one of the few medical schools in the United States at the time were poorly trained. In Europe, four-year medical schools were common, laboratory training was widespread, and an understanding of disease and infection existed. In contrast, the average medical student in the United States trained for two years or less and received almost no practical experience or laboratory work. Harvard University did not own a single stethoscope or microscope until after the war.

BIOGRAPHY

Sally Tompkins 1833–1916

BORN: Mathews County, Virginia

ROLE: Confederate nurse

When the Civil War began, Sally Tompkins turned a large house in Richmond, Virginia, into a hospital at her own expense. In September 1861, Confederate President Jefferson Davis issued an order closing all private hospitals, so that only hospitals under military control would be in use. However, he made Tompkins an officer in the Confederate cavalry—a move that allowed her hospital to continue, since Tompkins herself was now technically a member of the military. Tompkins was the only woman to hold a Confederate commission. "Captain Sally" cared for more than 1,000 patients, of whom only 73 died—an amazing record not equaled by any other hospital in the war.[7]

An amputation operation takes place outside a field hospital at the Battle of Gettysburg, 1863.

MEDICAL WORKERS

When the war began, the Union Army had a total of about 98 medical officers. The Confederacy had just 24. By 1865 about 13,000 Union doctors had served in the field and in the hospitals. In the Confederacy, about 4,000 medical officers and an unknown number of volunteers treated war casualties. In both the North and South, these men were assisted by thousands of women who donated their time and energy to help the wounded. More than 4,000 women served as nurses in Union hospitals, and Confederate women contributed much to the effort as well.

Although Civil War doctors were commonly referred to as "butchers" by their patients and newspapers, they managed to treat more than 10 million cases of injury and illness in just 48 months. About 110,000 Union and 94,000 Confederate men died of wounds received in battle. Every effort was made to treat wounded men within 48 hours. They were treated at field hospitals located far behind the front lines. Those who survived were then transported by unreliable and overcrowded ambulances—two-wheeled carts or four-wheeled wagons—to army hospitals located in nearby cities and towns.[8]

LIFE FOR AFRICAN AMERICANS

The issue of slavery was one of the main reasons the war was fought. This issue became more important after the Emancipation Proclamation of 1863 (see page 27). But what was the experience of African Americans during the conflict?

THE SOUTH

African Americans in the South remained slaves throughout the war. The Emancipation Proclamation changed nothing for most of them until the war was over and the Union was officially victorious. Slaves continued to have to work on plantations and in their owners' houses. As we have seen (see pages 8 to 11), life for slaves was brutal.

Some African Americans in the South were put to work supporting the war effort. African American men and women were forced to build fortifications and work as blacksmiths, nurses, boatmen, and laundresses. They also worked in factories, hospitals, and armories. However, many slaves took the opportunity to escape, particularly if the Union Army was nearby.

The Union was not prepared for the many people who came to them. Camps were hastily prepared, and many former slaves suffered in poor conditions. It was up to individual army commanders to cope. The idea developed that slaves who had been forced to contribute to the Confederate war effort were considered "**contraband** of war." By this logic, they could be taken by the Union Army and made free.[1]

THE NORTH

Although most Union states had rejected slavery, some states that stayed in the Union, like Maryland and Delaware, still allowed slavery—the Emancipation Proclamation only applied to the rebel Confederate states. African Americans in these states faced many of the same injustices as African Americans in the South. Life was not easy for African Americans in free northern states, either. Free blacks were often discriminated against by white people there.[2]

The New York draft riots of 1863

In 1863, just eight days after the victory of Gettysburg, draft riots broke out in New York City. The events of these days showed the extent to which racist attitudes still existed in the North.

Throughout the war, a draft required men to join the army—unless they were wealthy enough to purchase a substitute. This meant that rich people, generally whites, could pay a poorer person to do service in the army as a substitute. This practice was deeply resented by people who could not afford to pay substitutes—especially by some poor Irish Americans who did not want to risk their lives to free black slaves. These people also felt that African Americans would take their jobs while they were off serving in the army.[3]

Because of these growing resentments, riots broke out, and many African Americans were victimized. An orphanage was attacked and a nine-year-old girl was beaten to death. A hospital was targeted because it treated both black and white patients. Seventy-one British black sailors were chased through the streets, finding safety only when a French warship threatened to open fire on the rioters. Order was finally restored when Union troops marched into New York to enforce an end to the riots with artillery and bayonets. Nobody knows exactly how many people were killed.[4]

This image shows an African American man being attacked by a mob during the New York draft riots of 1863.

MILITARY EXPERIENCES

At the beginning of the war, free blacks were not allowed to join the Union Army. This changed after the Emancipation Proclamation. Black sailors could serve on Union ships, as they had for many years. Black army regiments started to be formed, starting with the 54th Massachusetts Regiment. They were led by white officers, and the troops received less pay than white regiments—although this was changed in 1864. In total, over 180,000 blacks served in the Union Army and 20,000 in the Union Navy. Just over 68,000 black people died as a result of the conflict, on all sides.[5]

In one of the best-known battles of the war, on July 18, 1863, the African American 54th Massachusetts Regiment attacked the Confederates' Fort Wagner, near Charleston, South Carolina. But they could not capture it, and their colonel, Robert Gould Shaw, was killed. They proved the bravery of black troops to everyone. One soldier, William H. Carney, was the first black soldier to win the Medal of Honor, the highest award for bravery in battle.[6]

A photo of Company B, 25th Infantry at Fort Snelling.

This 1890 picture shows the attack by the 54th Regiment on Fort Wagner in 1863.

IN ACTION: MILLIKEN'S BEND

This account by Captain M.M. Miller, a white officer of the 9th Louisiana (colored) regiment, describes the bravery of African American soldiers in the Union Army. The passage describes the Battle of Milliken's Bend, which happened on June 10, 1863, in Louisiana. It was part of the Siege of Vicksburg (see page 32):

Dear Aunt,
We were attacked here on June 7 by a brigade of Texas troops about 2,500 in number. We had about 600 men to withstand them, 500 of them negroes. I commanded Company I, Ninth Louisiana. We went into the fight with 33 men. I had 16 killed and 11 badly wounded. I felt sick at heart when I saw how my brave soldiers had been slaughtered, one with six wounds, all the rest with two or three, none less than two wounds. Two of my colored sergeants were killed, both brave, noble men; always prompt, vigilant, and ready for the fight. I never more wish to hear the expression, "The negroes wont fight." My soldiers are as brave, loyal, and patriotic as ever went into battle. The enemy charged us so close that we fought with our bayonets hand to hand. I have six broken bayonets to show how bravely my men fought. The Twenty-third Iowa (a white regiment) joined my men, and I declare truthfully that they had all fled before our regiment fell back, as we were all forced to do.[7]

WOMEN IN THE CIVIL WAR

We have already seen how women participated in the Civil War in the roles of nurses, cooks, and spies. Many also took on the roles of running their households, farms, stores, factories, and plantations while men were away at war.

Did you know?

Dr. Mary Walker, a surgeon in the Civil War, was awarded the nation's highest honor, the Medal of Honor, by President Andrew Johnson. The citation reads:

Dr. Mary E. Walker, a graduate of medicine, has rendered valuable service to the government. She was assigned to duty and served as an assistant surgeon in charge of female prisoners at Louisville, Kentucky. She has devoted herself with much patriotic zeal to the sick and wounded soldiers, both in the field and hospitals, to the detriment of her own health, and has endured hardships as a prisoner of war four months in a southern prison while acting as a surgeon.[1]

WOMEN IN COMBAT

Some women became soldiers and fought alongside men—a fact that many people realized, but which was rarely discussed at the time. These women tended to disguise themselves as men in order to fight. For example, Loreta Velazquez published her memoirs in 1876. She served the Confederacy as Lieutenant Harry Buford.

Most newspapers gave few details about individual women's army careers. For example, the **obituary** of Satronia Smith Hunt merely stated she **enlisted** in an Iowa regiment with her first husband. He died of battle wounds, but she apparently emerged from the war unharmed.

An 1896 story about Mary Stevens Jenkins, who died in 1881, tells an equally short tale. She enlisted in a Pennsylvania regiment when still a schoolgirl, remained in the army for two years, received several wounds, and was then discharged—without anyone ever realizing she was female. Some women wrote about their experiences; others fought and died without being known.[2]

LIFE FOR WOMEN IN THE SOUTH

Since the Civil War was fought in mostly Confederate areas, women in the South saw far more of the horrors of war and the destruction caused than women in the North.

However, at first, many plantation owners' wives and other wealthy women rejoiced that their states had finally broken from what they saw as the Union's hold. Many women encouraged their husbands and relatives to enlist by appealing to their sense of honor. The horrors of war would later cut down much of this enthusiasm. More affluent women also engaged in voluntary activities on the home front that proved vital to Confederate supplies.[3]

This romanticized painting called the Burial of Latane (a Confederate officer) is intended to show the nobility of southern women in the face of the deadly effects of war.

LIFE FOR WOMEN IN THE NORTH

During the Civil War, education in the North was limited for girls. Women also did not have the right to vote.

Women who worked outside of the home often worked as teachers or in other education-related jobs. If they did not work in education, they often worked in manufacturing. However, women who held jobs in manufacturing made half the pay that men earned working the same jobs. Women in industrial jobs suffered as the money they earned bought less and less as prices rose. Women whose husbands died during the war also faced many hardships because of the loss of their husbands' income.

Some women decided to improve the lives of the men fighting in the war, many of whom lived in poor conditions in camps. The U.S. Sanitary Commission used women to help raise money that would be used to help supply these men—although women were not allowed to hold any positions of significant authority within these organizations. Women were also hired in governmental offices, but not in high positions. Women served as secretaries and in low-level jobs.

Poorer women were often far more vulnerable to the war's devastation than were wealthy, slave-holding women. The wives and children of poor farmers had far fewer resources to draw from when their husbands left for war, and many experienced food shortages as early as 1862. Many women grew desperate by the war's midpoint. This desperation led to the widespread looting of stores and raids on warehouses by groups of poor women, often driven by hunger.

The civilian population faced its greatest trial during Sherman's 1864 March to the Sea (see page 40), when Union forces burned many homes in their path. As the soldiers made their way southeast, toward Savannah, they terrorized the women in their path. For many women, Sherman's March to the Sea increased their pleas for their men to abandon the army and return home.[4]

African American women in the South were still subject to the horrors of slavery during the Civil War. However, with many men away in the army, slaves' opportunity to escape to the North became much easier.

THE LOSS OF LOVED ONES

Many women's lives were devastated by the loss of loved ones—husbands, brothers, sons, and sweethearts. They also, especially in the South, lost homes and livelihoods. Here is one woman's account of the Union Army marching through Georgia:

> *November 19, 1864.*
>
> *Saw Mrs. Laura Perry in the road surrounded by her children, seeming to be looking for some one. She said she was looking for her husband, that old Mrs. Perry had just sent her word that the Yankees [Union Army] went to James Perry's the night before, plundered his house, and drove off all his stock. But like demons they rush in! My yards are full. To my smoke-house, my dairy, pantry, kitchen, and cellar, like famished wolves they come. The thousand pounds of meat in my smoke-house is gone in a twinkling, my flour, my meat, my lard, butter, eggs, pickles of various kinds, wine, jars, and jugs are all gone. My eighteen fat turkeys, chickens, and my young pigs, are shot down in my yard. They made a road through my back-yard, tearing down my fences and desolating my home. Deliberately doing it when there was no necessity for it. There were flames from burning buildings. The passing of Sherman's army by my place left me poorer by thirty thousand dollars than I was yesterday morning.*[5]

This shows the Confederate capital at Richmond, Virginia, after Union forces captured it in 1865.

THE END OF THE WAR

The final campaign of the Confederates' Army of Northern Virginia began March 25, 1865. Confederate General Robert E. Lee sought to break Union General Ulysses S. Grant's ever-tightening stranglehold at Petersburg, Virginia, by attacking the Union position at Fort Stedman. The attack failed.

Grant himself attacked a week later, on April 1 and 2. The Confederate defense broke, and Lee's much-smaller army abandoned Richmond and Petersburg. The Confederate retreat began to go southwest, as Lee sought to use the Richmond & Danville Railroad. But Grant moved too fast for Lee's plan to work. The Confederate Army was running out of supplies.

SURRENDER AT APPOMATTOX

On April 6, almost one-fourth of Lee's army was trapped and captured at Sayler's Creek, southwest of Petersburg. Lee led his remaining 30,000 men in a move across the Appomattox River. In the meantime, Grant, with four times as many men, sent General Phillip H. Sheridan's cavalry and most of two infantry corps to Appomattox Station. Reaching the railroad first, the Union forces blocked Lee's only line of advance.

On the morning of April 9, the Confederates found the Union Army to be too strong. That afternoon Lee met Grant in the front parlor of Wilmer McLean's home, near

Did you know?

The owner of the house in which General Lee surrendered was named Wilmer McLean. He was also the owner of the farm where the first shots of the First Battle of Bull Run (see page 22) were fired in 1861. McLean had bought the Appomattox house to avoid the war. But the war just seemed to follow him. Union officers looking for souvenirs stripped the room bare.[1]

Appomattox Court House, to discuss peace terms. Grant was very generous in his terms, allowing Confederate officers to keep their horses and sidearms. All soldiers were permitted to go home without interference. The Confederate Army surrendered on April 12. The fighting in the Civil War was officially over.[2]

"The rebels are our countrymen again."—General Grant, talking to his troops after the Confederate surrender at Appomattox

The following is an account of the surrender at Appomatox by Horace Porter, an officer in General Grant's army:

At a little before 4 o'clock General Lee shook hands with General Grant, bowed to the other officers. Lee signalled to his orderly to bring up his horse. The general stood on the lowest step and gazed sadly in the direction of the valley beyond where his army lay—now an army of prisoners. He smote his hands together a number of times in an absent sort of way; seemed not to see the group of Union officers in the yard who rose respectfully at his approach, and appeared unconscious of everything about him. All appreciated the sadness that overwhelmed him...

In this print General Lee (seated at the table in gray) is signing the Confederate surrender at the Appomattox court house in 1865. General Grant is seated to the right in blue. The 19th century print is based on eyewitness accounts.

THE ASSASSINATION OF PRESIDENT ABRAHAM LINCOLN

Just two days after General Lee's surrender, disaster struck for the Union. On the evening of April 14, 1865, President Abraham Lincoln was shot. He was at Ford's Theater, in Washington, D.C., at a special performance of the comedy *Our American Cousin*.

After the play was in progress, a figure with a small, short-barreled pistol stepped into the presidential box, aimed, and fired. The president slumped forward. The assassin, John Wilkes Booth, dropped the pistol and waved a dagger. Booth leapt from the balcony and caught the spur of his left boot on a flag draped over the rail, shattering a bone in his leg upon landing. Though injured, he rushed out the back door and disappeared into the night on horseback.

On April 26, Booth was shot and captured while hiding in a barn near Bowling Green, Virginia. He died later the same day. Four others were tried and found guilty of conspiracy with Booth to kill the President.[3]

Did you know?

- John Wilkes Booth was a very famous actor. When he jumped to the stage after the shooting, he is said to have shouted, "*Sic semper tyrannis*," which is Latin for "Thus always to tyrants." These words were said to have been first used by the murderers of Julius Caesar in Rome.
- Lincoln had a bodyguard that night, a policeman named John Parker. He was very unreliable and frequently in trouble. When Lincoln was watching the play, Parker moved to another box to get a better view. Later, he went to the Star Saloon next door to the theater with a footman and a coachman and did not return to the president's box. Amazingly, no action was taken against Parker.
- Secretary of State William H. Seward survived being stabbed several times by Lewis Paine. He later bought Alaska from Russia in 1867.
- Mary Surratt was the first woman ever to be executed on the orders of the U.S. government.

The execution of four accomplices of John Wilkes Booth in 1865.

They were hanged at the gallows of the Old Penitentiary, at Fort McNair near Washington, D.C., on July 7, 1865.[4]

- Mary Surratt, who owned a tavern in Washington and who had a son in the Confederate army and another son who was a Confederate spy who met with other spies, including Booth, at the tavern.
- George Atzerodt, a German immigrant, who was given the job of murdering Vice President Andrew Johnson but took no action.
- Lewis Paine, whose real name was Powell, who was supposed to murder Secretary of State William Seward but only succeeded in injuring him when he broke into his house and attacked him in bed.
- David Herold was originally supposed to kidnap Lincoln with Booth but the plan was changed. Herold went with Paine to kill Seward and fled with him. He was captured when Booth was fatally wounded.

RECONSTRUCTION IN THE SOUTH

When John Wilkes Booth assassinated President Lincoln, he thought that he was helping the South. Instead he made many northerners more hostile to the South. Moreover, President Lincoln had been ready to begin the process of reconciliation and had the political skills and support to do this.

The task of restoring the United States would fall to Lincoln's vice president, Andrew Johnson, a southerner who favored quick and easy "**Reconstruction**." This meant that the federal government set about rebuilding state governments and society in the former Confederacy. President Andrew Johnson tried to follow Lincoln's lenient policies and appointed new governors in the summer of 1865. Johnson quickly declared that the war goals of national unity and the ending of slavery had been achieved, so that reconstruction was completed.[5]

This school for freed slave children was built in the South after the Civil War and photographed in 1870.

Republicans in Congress refused to accept Johnson's terms, rejected the new members of Congress elected by the South, and in 1865–66 broke with the president. A large Republican victory in the 1866 Congressional elections in the North gave the Radical Republicans, who opposed being lenient to the South, enough control of Congress that they over-rode Johnson's vetoes and began what is called "Radical Reconstruction" in 1867. Congress removed the civilian governments in the South in 1867 and put the former Confederacy under the rule of the U.S. Army. The army conducted new elections in which the freed slaves could vote, while those who held leading positions under the Confederacy were temporarily denied the vote and could not run for office.

Three amendments to the U.S. Constitution were passed during the Reconstruction period. The 13th Amendment officially ended slavery and prohibited it for the future. The 14th Amendment said that former slaves were citizens and that everyone had equal protection under the law. The 15th Amendment guaranteed the vote for citizens regardless of race, color, or whether they had been slaves.[6]

THE COLLAPSE OF RECONSTRUCTION

The postwar Reconstruction process began with high ideals, but it collapsed into racism and corruption. The divisions and hatreds that had led to the Civil War did not disappear after the fighting stopped. Southern whites gradually regained political power, while southern blacks suffered. Even though African Americans had gained the right to vote, they were intimidated at the polls. The South became segregated, meaning black and white people were kept separate in public places such as restaurants and schools. Organizations in the South like the Ku Klux Klan formed.

The policy of Reconstruction was abandoned in 1877. White-dominated state governments in the South passed laws that prevented most African Americans and many poor whites from voting, through a combination of constitutional amendments, corruption, and electoral laws. These laws were known as "Jim Crow" laws. (The term "Jim Crow" was an insulting name for African Americans.) The laws included the segregation of public schools, public transportation, restrooms, restaurants, and drinking fountains for blacks and whites. The U.S. military was also segregated. Blacks and whites would remain segregated in many places for 100 years.

WHAT HAVE WE LEARNED?

The struggle over the rights of American Africans was not solved by the Civil War. As we have seen, the civil rights that former slaves gained and the right to vote did not last long. After the end of Reconstruction, Southern states passed laws about voter registration and poll taxes that made it very difficult for African Americans to vote. Combined with violence and intimidation from white supremacist groups like the Ku Klux Klan, this made it almost impossible for blacks in the South to use the vote.

THE FUTURE OF CIVIL RIGHTS

This racism continued into the 20th century. For example, during World War II (1939–45) African American soldiers were placed in segregated regiments and only allowed leave on different days than white soldiers, despite the fact that they fought for the same rights and values as their white counterparts. An aircraft unit known as the Tuskegee Airmen was spectacularly successful in air battles over Europe. It was made up of African American pilots and ground crew, but the senior officers were white.

Things started to change in the 1950s and 1960s. In 1955 a woman named Rosa Parks was arrested for sitting in a bus seat in Montgomery, Alabama, reserved for whites. This sparked widespread protest. Dr. Martin Luther King, Jr., became the respected leader of peaceful demands for civil rights. In 1964 Congress passed the Civil Rights Act, which made racial discrimination in public places, such as theaters, restaurants, and hotels, illegal. It also required employers to provide equal employment opportunities. The federal government cut off money if they found evidence of discrimination. Also, in the 20 years after World War II, Jim Crow laws were gradually swept away.[1]

THE CHANGING NATURE OF WARFARE AND INDUSTRY

The Civil War showed many major changes in warfare. Forces and supplies were moved rapidly by rail (the first time land movement was faster than water). Telegraph allowed for the possibility of instantaneous communication. And Industrial Age weapons were massively destructive. Huge artillery guns and mortars could fire explosive shells and shrapnel that slaughtered soldiers. The balls fired from Minié rifles were much more damaging than the smooth musket balls of the past. Some multishot repeating rifles were used during the war, as was an early type of machine gun. At sea, cannonballs from normal wooden ships simply bounced off the new ironclads.

At the same time, military tactics were very much the same as they had been 50 years before. Soldiers stood in the open and exchanged fire with their opponents. Trench warfare became more common in conflicts following the Civil War as soldiers realized they stood little chance of survival in open battles.

The Civil War also shows us that economies based on industry are more powerful than those based on agriculture. The North could afford to pay more soldiers. It could produce and buy more weapons. When materials were lost or destroyed, they could be replaced. The North had more railroads and so could move large numbers of troops and their supplies. The North could also afford to build a large navy and so enforce the blockade, which further weakened the Confederate economy. At the end of the war, Confederate armies were often ragged, hungry, and low on ammunition.[2]

LEADERSHIP

Differences can lead to hatred and intolerance if they are not discussed. Still, in 1860 South Carolina was probably determined to secede and take most of the other southern states with it, no matter what compromises Lincoln or other northern leaders might have tried to make. President Lincoln wanted to restore the Union and lead the United States in a new start. He was not inclined to punish the South for its rebellion. But his assassination had unintended consequences. When he was killed, hard-line Republicans took control of Congress, and the South was duly punished.

The defeated South harbored deep resentment for many years. This was because southerners felt that their states' rights had been violated, and that their traditions and culture had been unfairly attacked. They also resented the way they were treated during the period of Reconstruction.

TIMELINE

1860 November 6	Abraham Lincoln is elected president.
December 20	South Carolina secedes from the Union.
1861 January–February	Mississippi, Florida, Alabama, Georgia, Louisiana, and Texas secede.
February	The secessionist states create a Confederate government, based in Montgomery, Alabama. The South begins to seize federal forts.
February 9	Jefferson Davis is named provisional president of the Confederacy.
March 4	Lincoln becomes U.S. president. He hopes to resolve the national crisis without warfare.
April 12–13	Confederate forces attack Fort Sumter, near Charleston, South Carolina.
April 17	Virginia secedes.
May 6	Arkansas secedes.
May 20	North Carolina secedes.
May 21	Richmond, Virginia, is named the Confederate capital.
June	Four slave states stay in the Union: Delaware, Kentucky, Maryland, and Missouri.
June 8	Tennessee secedes.
July	The Union begins a naval blockade of the South.
July 21	The First Battle of Bull Run (First Battle of Manassas) is fought in Virginia.
1862 January 27	President Lincoln takes action against the secessionist states by issuing a war order to fight the Confederacy.
March	The Peninsular Campaign begins, a major Union offensive in Virginia.
March 9	The Battle of Hampton Roads is fought at sea, off Virginia.
April 6–7	The Battle of Shiloh is fought in Hardin County, Tennessee.

April 25	The Union begins a naval attack on New Orleans.
May	General "Stonewall" Jackson defeats Union forces.
August 28–30	The Second Battle of Bull Run (Second Battle of Manassas) is fought in Virginia.
September 17	The Battle of Antietam is fought in Maryland.
December 13	The Battle of Fredericksburg is fought in Virginia.
1863 January 1	President Lincoln issues the Emancipation Proclamation.
May 1–May 5	The Battle of Chancellorsville is fought in Virginia.
May 22–July 4	The Siege of Vicksburg is fought in Mississippi.
June 7	The Battle of Milliken's Bend is fought in Louisiana.
July 1–3	The Battle of Gettysburg is fought in Pennsylvania.
July 18	The Battle of Fort Wagner is fought near Charleston.
September 19–20	The Battle of Chickamauga is fought in Georgia.
November 19	President Lincoln delivers the Gettysburg Address.
November 23–25	The Battle of Chattanooga is fought in Tennessee. Union forces push Confederate troops away from Chattanooga. The victory sets the stage for General Sherman's Atlanta Campaign.
1864 May	General Sherman's Atlanta Campaign begins.
May 5–7	Grant's Battle of the Wilderness is fought in Virginia.
May 8–19	The Battle of Spotsylvania Court House is fought in Virginia.
June 9	The First Battle of Petersburg is fought in Virginia.
July	Confederate troops approach Washington, D.C.
November 8	Abraham Lincoln is reelected president.
November 15–December 21	General Sherman leads the March to the Sea.
1865 February	Sherman's forces march through North and South Carolina.
March 25	The Siege of Petersburg ends.
April	The Union Army captures Richmond, Virginia.
April 12	Confederate forces surrender at Appomattox, Virginia.
April 14	President Lincoln is shot.
April 15	President Lincoln dies.

GLOSSARY

abolition belief or cause supporting the abolishment, or end, of slavery

abolitionist person who supported or pursued the abolishment of slavery

amendment addition to the U.S. Constitution

amputate to surgically cut off badly damaged or infected parts of the human body

armament weapons

artillery big guns which fire metal projectiles like solid shot or explosive shells

bayonet pointed or edged knife or sword that is attached to a rifle to stab at an opponent who is close by

blockade trying to weaken an opponent by not letting supplies of help into or out of a port or a town

brigade large group of soldiers made up of smaller groups all under the overall command of a general

casualty someone wounded or killed in a conflict

cavalry soldiers who travel and fight on horseback

civil rights the rights of a person that should protect them from unacceptable interference from the state or other groups of people

civilian someone who is not in a military organization

colony group of people who live in a new land but are controlled by a far-away parent country. In North America in the 18th century, there were 13 original colonies set up by British immigrants who had moved there in the 17th and early 18th centuries.

compromise deal made when two sides come to an agreement, both giving up some of their ideas in order to ensure there is no further argument

Confederacy name given to the states that seceded from the Union in 1861 and set up their own government

Confederate someone or something belonging to the Confederacy

consecrate make holy

contraband goods being moved that are illegal

corps the second biggest army unit

counterintelligence spies who have the job of finding out what the spies of the other side are doing and then stopping them from succeeding

discriminate single out a person or group for different, unequal treatment

draw contest, like a battle, in which there is no winner or loser. The sides are evenly matched.

enlist volunteer to join a military organization

export send goods away to another country

federal a form of government where power is shared between a central government and several other regional governments. In the U.S., the central government was in Washington D.C., and the regional governments in each state. Because the central government was that of the Union or North, federal was often used to describe that side in the Civil War.

flank attack attacking from the side of an army

fugitive someone who runs away from the law

garrison group of soldiers that permanently live in a town or fortress

hallow make holy

immoral act or belief that goes against what is normally considered to be the right thing

import bring goods into one country from another country

industry a form of economic production where goods are made out of raw materials

infantry soldiers who travel (not always) and fight on foot

ironclad a type of naval ship that is made of wood with a covering of iron sheets

loot to steal things during military actions. Also refers to the things that are stolen.

memoir someone's memories of events, generally written down

Minié rifle a type of rifle which used a lead bullet that spun in the barrel, which made it go further and be more accurate. Named after a French soldier who invented the bullet.

mortar short-barreled, short-range gun that fires shells high into the air

musket an old fashioned (in 1861) type of long barrelled soldiers' gun. It fired a round lead ball. It was short ranged and inaccurate and needed the gunpowder being cleaned from the barrel frequently.

obituary piece of writing that describes the life of someone who has died

overseer supervisor who was in charge of slaves. An overseer, rather than the actual slave owners, made slaves work. Overseers were often people who were the sons of white slave owners and black slave mothers.

plantation a farm, generally large, where only one or two crops are grown, mainly to be sold

rear guard last troops in an army to leave a battle

reconnaissance soldiers going out to discover where the enemies are

Reconstruction the Union plan to rebuild the economy, government, and society of the Confederacy when the war was over

regiment unit of soldiers, commanded by a colonel, comprising up to a thousand troops

score old-fashioned word meaning the number 20

secede break away to form another nation

secession act of breaking away to form another nation

segregation making one group of people live, often in worse conditions, apart from another group

shell outer casing of steel or iron with explosive inside that is fired from an artillery gun. It bursts in the air or on contact and sends chunks of its casing to destroy its target.

siege trying to capture a place by surrounding it, not letting anything in or out and by bombarding it with artillery

surplus more than what is needed

traitor person who works for an enemy

treason the acts of a traitor by helping an enemy against his own side

trench ditch in the ground to give soldiers some protection against enemy fire

turret part of a ship (or tank) where guns are loaded and fired. Heavily protected by metal armor plate. Turrets generally rotate so that the guns can be fired in most directions.

Union the name given to the United States when they all agreed to share a central government for national issues. When the Confederacy broke away, the North retained the name Union. The restoration of the Union was one of the great war aims of President Abraham Lincoln and the Northern side.

NOTES ON SOURCES

A War of Brother Against Brother (pages 4–5)

1. Teaching American History in South Carolina Project http://www.teachingushistory.org/lessons/Campbellpapers.htm.
2. Burke Davis, *The Civil War, Strange and Fascinating Facts*, (New York: Fairfax Press, 1982).
3. Philip Katcher and Rick Scollins, *Flags of the American Civil War* (Reed International Books Limited, 1992).
4. Veterans Today 2009, http://www.veteranstoday.com/2009/02/16/albert-woolson-the-last-living-civil-war-veteran/.

Buildup to War (pages 6–15)

1. PBS, "Two Nations' Identities: Looking Forward and Looking Back," *The U.S.-Mexican War*, http://www.pbs.org/kera/usmexicanwar/resources/video_library.html.
2. PBS, Manifest Destiny, http://www.pbs.org/kera/usmexicanwar/prelude/md_introduction.html
3. Abolition, http://www.loc.gov/exhibits/african/afam005.html
4. Spartacus Educational, http://www.spartacus.schoolnet.co.uk/USAStubman.htm
5. Harriet Jacobs (writing as Linda Brent)"Incidents in the Life of a Slave Girl". First published January 1861 privately in Boston Mass. Republished Jan 2010 Indo-European Publishing.
6. Frederick Douglass, "Life and Times of Frederick Douglass, Written by Himself", Cleveland, Hamilton, Rewell & Co. 1883.
7. Frederick Douglass, "My Bondage and My Freedom" 1855. Republished Jan 2010 Indo-European Publishing.
8. Missouri Compromise, http://www.loc.gov/rr/program/bib/ourdocs/Missouri.html
9. PBS, The Compromise of 1850, http://www.pbs.org/wgbh/aia/part4/4p2951.html
10. Catalogs.com 2007. http://www.catalogs.com/info/history/famous-women-in-history.html
11. http://millercenter.org/president/events/05_30
12. http://www.pbs.org/wgbh/aia/part4/4p2952.html
13. Spartacus Educational, http://www.spartacus.schoolnet.co.uk/USAlincoln.htm

Secession and the Battle of Fort Sumter (pages 16–21)

1. Jefferson Davis Facts.com http://jeffersondavisfacts.com/
2. Fort Sumter, http://www.nps.gov/hps/abpp/battles/sc001.htm
3. http://www.civilwarhome.com/anderson.htm
4. http://www.civilwarhome.com/CMHsumter.htm
5. The US Library of Congress, http://memory.loc.gov/ammem/tafthtml/tafthome.html

A Nation at War (pages 22–31)

1. http://americancivilwar.com/north/Union_Generals/General_Irvin_McDowell.html
2. http://www.whitehouse.gov/about/presidents/ulyssessgrant
3. Civil War Cavalry, http://ehistory.osu.edu/uscw/features/regimental/cavalry.cfm
4. http://www.historynet.com/weaponry-the-rifle-musket-and-the-mini-ball.htm
5. http://www.historyofwar.org/articles/battles_bullrun2.html
6. Antietam National Battlefield, http://www.nps.gov/ancm/index.htm
7. http://www.archives.gov/exhibits/featured_documents/emancipation_proclamation/

8. CivilWarHome.com, http://www.civilwarhome.com/leebio.htm
9. CivilWarHome.com, http://www.civilwarhome.com/jackbio.htm
10. Absolom A. Harrison 1862 www.civilwarhome.com/harrisonlettersintro.htm
11. R.W. Burt 1863 http://my.ohio.voyager.net/~lstevens/burt/burtdiar.html

The Tide Turns: Victory for the Union (pages 32–43)

1. http://www.historyofwar.org/articles/battles_vicksburg.html
2. http://www.army.mil/gettysburg/flash.html
3. American Rhetoric, 2001-2011, http://www.americanrhetoric.com/speeches/gettysburgaddress.htm
4. Battle Summary: Chickamauga, GA http://www.nps.gov/hps/abpp/battles/ga004.htm
5. http://www.civilwar.org/battlefields/the-wilderness.html
6. http://www.archives.gov/southeast/education/resources-by-state/atlanta-campaign.html
7. Robert Underwood Johnson (Ed.) "Battles and Leaders of the Civil War" published Pennsylvania 1887. (originally published in Century Magazine).
8. The Appomattox Campaign, http://clccharter.org/kurt1/Civil%20War/Appomattox%20Campaign/Appomattoxhome.html
9. History.com, http://www.history.com/topics/william-t-sherman
10. http://www.civilwar.org/education/history/biographies/david-farragut.html
11. Friends of the Hunley, http://www.hunley.org/
12. http://www.historyofwar.org/articles/battles_hampton_roads.html

People in the Civil War (pages 44–51)

1. http://www.civilwarhome.com/watiebio.htm
2. http://www.americancivilwar.org.uk/
3. http://www.east-buc.k12.ia.us/98_99/CW/spies/title.htm
4. National Geographic, 1996-2011, http://kids.nationalgeographic.com/kids/stories/peopleplaces/harriettubman/
5. http://www.centennialofflight.gov/essay/Lighter_than_air/Civil_War_balloons/LTA5.htm
6. George Skoch "Inside Andersonville: An Eyewitness Account of the Civil War's Most Infamous Prison" Published *Civil War Times* 2007.
7. Keppel Hagerman, 1996, "Dearest of Captains: a biography of Sally Louisa Tompkins" (White Stone, Virginia. Brandylane Publishers, 1996)
8. Civil War Home, http://www.civilwarhome.com/civilwarmedicine.htm

Life for African Americans (pages 52–55)

1. http://www.pbs.org/wgbh/americanexperience/features/timeline/lincolns-soldiers/
2. http://lcweb2.loc.gov/ammem/aaohtml/exhibit/aopart4.html
3. http://www.press.uchicago.edu/Misc/Chicago/317749.html
4. http://www.vny.cuny.edu/draftriots/Intro/draft_riot_intro_set.html
5. http://www.pbs.org/wgbh/americanexperience/features/timeline/lincolns-soldiers/
6. http://www.civilwar.org/education/history/biographies/robert-gould-shaw.html
7. Letter from Captain M M Miller, 1863. United States War Department. "The War of the Rebellion: A Compilation of the Official Records of the Union and Confederate Armies." Series III, Volume 3. Washington: Government Printing Office, 1880-1901. At Website http://www.lwfaaf.net/cwdata/ltr_mmm.htm

Women in the Civil War (pages 56–59)

1. http://www.northnet.org/stlawrenceaauw/walker.htm
2. http://www.archives.gov/publications/prologue/1993/spring/

women-in-the-civil-war-1.html
3. http://www.historycentral.com/CivilWar/AMERICA/south.html
4. Dolly Sumner Lunt, "A Woman's Wartime Journal, An Account of the Passage Over a Georgia Plantation of Sherman's Army on the March to the Sea, as Recorded in the Diary of Dolly Sumner Lunt. (1918) used in Buel, Clarence, and Robert U. Johnson (eds.), Battles and Leaders of the Civil War, Vol.IV (originally published in Century Magazine, 1888; reprint ed., 1982)
5. *Ibid*

The End of the War (pages 60–65)

1. Verbal information from Mr Robin Wichard, expert Civil War historian and (Confederate) re-enactor.
2. http://www.nps.gov/apco/index.htm
3. http://memory.loc.gov/ammem/alhtml/alrintr.html
4. http://law2.umkc.edu/faculty/projects/ftrials/lincolnconspiracy/lincolnaccount.html
5. http://americanhistory.si.edu/presidency/timeline/pres_era/3_656.html
6. http://www.ushistory.org/documents/amendments.htm

What Have We Learned? (pages 66–67)

1. http://www.civilrights.org/resources/
2. http://www.cgsc.edu/carl/resources/csi/gabel4/gabel4.asp

BIBLIOGRAPHY

BOOKS

Catton, Bruce. *American Heritage: A Short History of the Civil War.* New York: Dell Publishing, 1963.

Heidler, David Stephen, Jeanne T. Heidler, and David J. Coles, eds. *Encyclopedia of the American Civil War: A Political, Social, and Military History*. Santa Barbara, Calif.: ABC-CLIO, 2000.

Kagan, Neil, and Steve Hyslop. *Eyewitness to the Civil War: The Complete History from Secession to Reconstruction*. Washington, DC: National Geographic, 2006.

Miller, Francis Trevelyan, Robert S. Lanier, and Henry Steele Commanger, eds. *The Photographic History of the Civil War*. 10 vols. New York: The Review of Reviews, 1912.

Time–Life Books. *The Civil War*. 28 vols. Alexandria, Va.: Time–Life Books, 1987.

Ward, Geoffrey C., Ric Burns, and Ken Burns. *The Civil War: An Illustrated History*. New York: Knopf, 1990.

WEBSITES

The Library of Congress
www.loc.gov

The American Civil War Home Page
www.civilwarhome.com

The American Civil War.com
www.americancivilwar.com

Spartacus Educational
www.spartacus.schoolnet.co.uk

The Civil War Home Page
www.civil-war.net

Eyewitness to History
www.eyewitnesstohistory.com

FIND OUT MORE

BOOKS

Heidler, David Stephen, Jeanne T. Heidler, and David J. Coles, eds. *Encyclopedia of the American Civil War: A Political, Social, and Military History*. Santa Barbara, Calif.: ABC-CLIO, 2000.

Kagan, Neil, and Steve Hyslop. *Eyewitness to the Civil War: The Complete History from Secession to Reconstruction*. Washington, D.C.: National Geographic, 2006.

Ward, Geoffrey C., Ric Burns, and Ken Burns. *The Civil War: An Illustrated History*. New York: Knopf, 1990.

WEBSITES

www.loc.gov

Visit the website of the Library of Congress. This is the official U.S. government records library, containing a huge collection of original documents and pictures.

www.civilwarhome.com

This huge Civil War website is easy to navigate. Sections include an overview of the war, a list of battles, biographies, medical facts, essays, figures for casualties, letters, naval war details, other site links, strategy and tactics, army details, and stories of army life.

www.americancivilwar.com

This is another very large site about the Civil War that includes indexes, original works, biographies, direct access to battle information, a Kids' Zone, and resource materials.

www.civil-war.net

This website provides thousands of pages, including interactive features, a links database, official records, books and movie recommendations, photos database, battle maps, Union regimental histories, figures for regimental losses, biographies, census information, and personal collections.

www.eyewitnesstohistory.com

This general history site has a section on the Civil War, including letters and diaries from people who were there at the time.

DVDS

The Civil War (Hollywood, Calif.: PBS Home Video, distributed by Paramount Home Entertainment, 2011; originally shown 1990).
A television miniseries by the acclaimed documentary filmmaker Ken Burns, this is a very detailed and thorough account of the war using contemporary photographs and actors speaking the actual words that people like Lincoln, Lee, and Grant said or wrote at the time.

Gettysburg (Burbank, Calif.: Warner Home Video, 2000; originally shown 1993).
Originally made as a television miniseries, this examines the events of the Battle of Gettysburg in great detail. The armies are played by reenactors whose hobby is to accurately re-create events from the Civil War.

Glory (Culver City, Calif.: Columbia TriStar Home Video, 2006; originally released 1989).
This movie is one of the few films to depict the participation of African American soldiers in the Civil War. It draws from the letters of Robert Gould Shaw, the 25-year-old son of Boston abolitionists who volunteered to command the all-black 54th Massachusetts Regiment.

The Red Badge of Courage (Burbank, Calif.: Warner Home Video, 2003; originally released 1951).
This movie is based on a book written in 1894 by Stephen Crane. It tells the story of a young man about to go into battle for the first time. He worries about how he will behave—will he be a coward? It stars Audie Murphy, who in real life was the most decorated U.S. soldier in World War II.

TOPICS TO RESEARCH

If you want to find out more about the Civil War and its causes, you could try researching the following topics:

- slavery and the slave trade, including reading Uncle Tom's Cabin by Harriet Beecher Stowe
- Sherman's March to the Sea
- families split by the Civil War
- the Civil War archives of the Library of Congress.

INDEX